M000168214

ABILENE LANDMARKS

An Illustrated Tour

ABILENE LANDMARKS
An Illustrated Tour

by
Donald S. Frazier and Robert F. Pace

Photographs by Steve Butman

State ★ House
Press

McMurry University
Abilene, Texas

in partnership with

PRESERVE
AMERICA
Explore and Enjoy Our Heritage

Cataloging-in-Publication Data Applied for

Copyright © 2008 State House Press

All Rights Reserved

State House Press
P.O. Box 818
Buffalo Gap, Texas 79508
www.mcwhiney.org

No part of this book may be reproduced in any form or by any means without permission in writing from State House Press.

Printed in Canada

ISBN: 978-193333730-2

Book designed by
Rosenbohm Graphic Design

TABLE OF CONTENTS

TOUR THREE−1930-1959:

TOUR FOUR—1960-2006:

Since its founding in 1996, the Grady McWhiney Research Foundation has been dedicated to educating the next generation of Americans, especially about the history of their community, state, and nation. To that end, this organization has involved scores of college students, area teachers, and public school kids in various projects over the years that have helped preserve, protect, and perpetuate their heritage. Now there are dozens of historical projects across the country—and across town—that have been supported, developed, and enhanced along the way.

The idea for this book came out of a Fall 2004 history research and writing class at McMurry University. We wanted the students in that class to be able to research and write about the histories of the buildings that surround them in Abilene. We also issued the same challenge to a group of honors students at McMurry in the Spring 2008 semester.

To create the list of buildings that would be appropriate and representative of the processes of Abilene's history, we enlisted a panel of experts—Dr. Rob Sledge, Abilene historian; Ruby Perez, then Executive Director of the Abilene Preservation League; and Rick Weatherl, historic preservation architect. In addition, we also took in hundreds of suggestions from others, including most notably, Steve Butman, who is a member of the Abilene Historic Landmarks Committee, and countless others. Many worthy properties did not make it into this book, unfortunately. In fact, we were amazed at the number of buildings that do remain from the very early days of Abilene. To include them all would have been unfeasible.

The students did a great job in their efforts, but producing their work as a book was not going to be a possibility until we found funding to do the job right. Starting in 2004, the Abilene Convention and Visitor's Bureau and the Abilene Cultural Affairs Council approached us about partnering to achieve a national designation for the city based on the strength of the cultural and heritage efforts in town.

The program they had in mind, Preserve America, is an executive branch initiative that "encourages and supports community efforts to preserve and enjoy the priceless cultural and natural heritage of the United States." Other goals of the initiative include "a greater shared knowledge about the nation's past, strengthened regional identities and local pride, increased local participation in preserving the country's cultural and natural heritage assets, and support for the economic vitality of our communities." Laura Bush, First Lady of the United States, is the Honorary Chair of Preserve America. Ideal communities for this recognition include those that "protect and celebrate their heritage, use their historic assets for economic development and community revitalization, and encourage people to experience and appreciate local historic resources through education and heritage tourism programs." Abilene received that designation in 2005.

With this award in hand, this same team successfully applied for a grant sponsored by Preserve America. This book, a telling of Abilene's history through the buildings that compose its cityscape, is one of the projects supported—in part—by this effort. Some individuals certainly bear mentioning. Kelly Thompson and Nanci Liles at the

9

Abilene Convention and Visitor's Bureau took a keen interest in this book. Betty Lou Miller Giddens let us use her extensive Abilene postcard collection to help illustrate the book.

In the process of crafting this project, we made a host of amazing and interesting discoveries about the built environment that is our hometown. One of the most intriguing discoveries, though, involved the use of pretty old and

conventional preservation research methodology married to very high tech solutions. In the nineteenth century—just about the time of Abilene's founding, the Sanborn Fire Insurance Company of New York began creating maps of America's cities that included not only street grids, but also the layout of buildings on their lots, and the composition of their construction. Their hope was to make the best guess on insurance premiums based on having a deep knowledge of the actual stuff from which these communities were made. There are Sanborn maps of Abilene ranging from 1885 to 1950, and there are on-line links available through the Abilene Library Consortium.

When viewed consecutively, these images reveal a town spreading out over time, creating a distinctive footprint on the planet. There are thousands of stories that wait to be told by a careful study of the maps. In the early days there were cotton gins and lumberyards all around

town. In 1925, a "Non-Progressive Christian" congregation met on Locust between South Seventh and South Sixth. What happened to these businesses, these people, and why?

More intriguing though, is to have these line drawings on your computer monitor while using satellite view programs like Google Earth to provide a present-day view. There, as seen from space, are the fabulous homes and the common houses, the ultra-sleek structures and the venerable old workhorses. Many—most—of the building outlines marked on the Sanborn maps have gone away.

But not all. There, tucked away in this city's neighborhoods, are the old landmarks, most still serving the roles uncelebrated, but still a fabric of this place.

When zooming out on the satellite view in Google Earth, Abilene takes on a distinctive outline. There, on the tan canvas created by the West Texas prairies, sits something that looks for all the world like a giant thumbprint, with its twisting creeks and irregular lakes, it streets and highways serving as the dermal ridges.

To us, it is a fitting metaphor. Abilene, when viewed from the heavens, takes on the unique signature of a people and a place that created and still calls this part of America home.

Donald S. Frazier &
Robert F. Pace
McMurry University
Abilene, Texas
February 2008

Marks on the Land

by Donald S. Frazier

Iron-rimmed wagon wheels make a scuffling, crunching sort of noise as they churn away the miles of the Texas prairie. Lathered horses—or more likely mules—with heads lowered against their burden, continue their monotonous labor with clopping hooves and creaking leather adding to the gentle rhythm of travel. Rattling wood and groaning timber, with the occasional high-pitched squeak and ping of metal under pressure, under friction, adds an accent to the harmony. A melody line of puffing wind and fluffing canvas adds an ethereal finish to the pioneer song and repeats itself with only the slightest of variation.

Above, the crystal vault of heaven. Wisps of clouds, high up, mark the limits of the blue and give definition and depth to the curved cerulean canvas.

Right and left lay the dun-colored plains.

Blue over buff.

Sunrise to sunset, the days blend together with a pattern that comforts and dulls, fatigues and fortifies. The breeze smells like fresh grass and old dust, the secret taste of sweat and salt a reminder of the tough days ahead.

Sophie A. Poe, heading onto the Texas plains, knew the routine of prairie travel, and it unsettled her. "I felt as if I were alone on a vast sea" she mused, "and wondered where my next harbor was going be." Lurching her way across a vast khaki ocean, buffeted by breezes and gusts of hot wind, Sophie longed for a glimpse of the familiar, a reminder of home—a guarantee that this great vastness would not swallow her whole. She craved familiar landmarks.

A generation before, Lieutenant Clinton Lear, of the Fifth Infantry, accompanied a column of troops out onto these West Texas plains to create a mark where once there had been none. He, too, surveyed the sameness stretching around him, horizon to horizon, and pondered the seemingly hopeless task ahead. His job was to establish a presence in this vast landscape, to make a smudge on the land that signaled the arrival of people like him who would change the very look and feel of this monotone expanse. The prospects of doing that seemed hopeless to him.

"We are like the dove after the deluge," he wrote back east to his wife that autumn of 1851. "Not one green sprig can we find to indicate that this was ever intended for man to inhabit. Indeed, I cannot imagine that God ever intended white man to occupy such a barren waste." Even so, he followed his orders and watched as sons of America and Europe, native-born and immigrant, fanned out across an unspectacular slope and cut into the earth with spade and pick, stake and pin. Within hours a village of canvas spread out where once there had been none, the first stirrings of the appropriately dubbed Fort Phantom Hill.

Within months dozens of stone chimneys climbed skyward and a regular, orderly cluster of rock and log buildings broke up the terrain and imposed symmetry onto the disordered chaos of the once-trackless wilderness. The soldiers brought familiarity onto the plains.

They imposed their mark on the land. While the fort only lasted three years, the skeletal remains of its buildings changed the landscape forever.

From that day onward, travelers across this prairie marked their progress by how close they were to the chimneys. The hills on the horizon seemed always just out of reach. The grasslands nearby provided nothing for the mind's eye to cling to. But the chimneys, ah, those were real—tangible—at hand. When John Warren Butterfield, a partner in the later and much more famous American Express company, won the contract to establish a mail route from St. Louis to San Francisco, he blazed a trail across the southern plains that passed through the ruins of Phantom Hill. Passengers making that excruciating trip from Missouri had, when the chimneys hove into site, put nearly 900 miles and 237 hours between them and the Mississippi.

Of course, the rocks of Phantom Hill also meant that that an additional 1,800 miles and nearly 475 hours lay ahead.

Those rutted tracks were by no means the first to mark the region. The Indians and Spanish had traversed these plains well before, marking their trails by hills and streams. Those paths had been infrequently used and, as a result were subtle, in harmony with the landscape rather than a clear intrusion. These newcomers and their wagons, though, using man-made features to mark their way, no longer worked with nature but instead dominated it with signs of their passing.

The railroad cut the land forever in 1880. Like the people who had come before, the gandy dancers of the Texas and Pacific Railroad brought a rhythmic song of transformation that sculpted this region. Their work songs echoed the coming of a new age.

Pick an' shovel...huh,
am so heavy...huh,
Heavy as lead...huh,
heavy as lead...huh
Pickin', shov'lin'...huh
pickin', shov'lin'...huh
Till I'm dead...huh
till I'm dead...

When these workers approached this endless grassland they planted towns in their wake as intentional scuffs on the landscape. Their tasks, by nature, answered the demands of engineering and economics as they made their way across the country. Behind lay the gunmetal gray tracks of their work and the blossoms of settlement. Ahead lay terrain yet to be broken to their will. When the time came to plant yet another settlement, and to differentiate one spot of track as unique from the others, the gandy dancers pounded a stake into the heart of this part of the prairie. One post, mile 407, would mark the land to this day, for around it, for miles in every direction, would arise the city of Abilene.

Planners laid out a simple grid based on the "Philadelphia system" typical of most railroad-manufactured towns. Streets running east to west parallel to the tracks would be numbered according to their distance from the right of way, and designated either "north or south." Streets running perpendicular to the rails would bear the names of trees, flowers, and fruits.

A reporter for the *Dallas Herald* gave the town's name as "Abilene" in the December 23 edition of the paper, attributing the moniker to Grenville M. Dodge, the chief engineer and president of the Texas and Pacific Construction Company. Others assert Clabe Merchant or J.T. Berry first coined the town name. Nevertheless, the name seemed appropriate. Abilene was, after all, one of the kingdoms named in St. Luke's account of the birth of Jesus and referred to a city on a fertile and grassy plain in Roman Syria, a dozen and a half miles northwest of Damascus. Of course, another American town by the same name had already sprung up in Kansas and, as the terminal for the Chisholm Trail, had been a boom town and headline grabber during the rowdy heyday of cattle drives. But that was last decade and 565 miles away. Dodge figured there was plenty of room on the Great Plains for two Abilenes. His, after all, would be the one that stuck, the one people would remember. Railroad pitch men hawked the new town as "The Future Great City of West Texas."

The first locomotive chuffed its way to mile post 407 on Sunday, February 27, 1881, passing by a growing village of tents springing up among the surveying stakes and chalk lines marking the boundaries of the settlement's invisible streets, alleys, and roads. A few yards from the tracks, Presbyterians and fellow faithful gathered to mark the Lord's Day and to organize the town's first church. With plans in place and newsprint inked, all that was left to do was begin the town in earnest by selling off parcels of sod to Abilene's charter citizens. Investors began buying their own claim to Abilene on Tuesday, March 15, 1881. The first town lots sold, on the northwest corner of North Second and Pine, went John T. Berry, soon followed by the purchases of the other 2,000 people at the auction. To the north and south, plats bounded the original townsite to North Tenth Street and South Ninth Street. North of the tracks, Osage street was its western margin and Sassafras the eastern. South of the tracks, Vine marked the western limit and Apple the east. By sunset the first residents of the city owned their own piece of Texas. They would soon add their marks to the land.

The rise of the town over the next half-dozen years followed a predictable pattern. Loads of boards and hardware flew away from the railroad sidings and the three major lumber yards in town—Bill Cameron's on either side of North Second between Walnut and Mesquite, John R. Jones's occupying the block of South First between Pecan and Locust, and R. H. Parker's on the block of South Second between Sycamore and Elm. For months the sounds of hammers and saws carried on the wind as simple wooden rectangles rose up to take their place on the prairie horizon. A trackside hotel and dining room between Cypress and Pine streets marked the western margin of the economic center of gravity, and a cluster of a dozen false front clapboard stores, rooming houses, and saloons huddled shoulder-to-shoulder behind it along North First and up either side of Pine Street for another block.

The streets were dusty in drought, and boggy in flood; even so, residents kept coming. By 1884 some 2,500 people called Abilene home, a population best described as young and white. Only about six per cent of the residents were Asian, Hispanic, or African American. One early observer noted that the average businessman was about thirty-five-years old and had come to this part of Texas from all across the nation, but mostly from the South and Midwest.

During the construction frenzy of early Abilene, saloons and rooming houses outnumbered churches. One structure, though, made a statement. By 1885 an Episcopal house of worship made of stone rose on the northeast corner of Orange and North Second, a symbol of the timelessness and unshakable nature of faith on this Texas frontier.

Other more industrial builds rose up. Farmers and stockmen from the surrounding countryside loaded their wagons and freighted to Abilene to sell their wares to businessmen there, or shipped them by rail to customers further a field. Commission merchants opened up shops near the tracks, including Theodore Heyck, who erected a colossal two-story warehouse facility at the western corner of North First and Cypress to store the region's wool harvest. Grocers and dry goods merchants, intermingled with livery stables and wagon yards, clustered along South First between Oak and Chestnut and across the tracks from the railroad hotel. John Estes dominated the skyline a mile east of the town and south of the tracks when he built his combination flour mill and cotton gin, all driven by a noisy steam engine. Abilene would be the great warehousing and shipping center through which the bounty of the surrounding land would head to market.

The Taylor County seat of government also relocated to Abilene, abandoning Buffalo Gap hidden away in the tree-shaded hills to the south in favor of the bustling board metropolis arising on the prairie. An impressive Second Republic style courthouse, typical of public structures in the American Midwest, arose on the block of South Third between Oak and Pecan, anchoring the southern precincts of Abilene's downtown commercial district. Abilene now threw a longer shadow on the prairie as a result of this three-story Victorian temple of justice and its crowning clock tower, presiding over a growing village of two-story industrial buildings, hotels, and warehouses.

The center of town soon wore an arc of houses on its western rim, the homes of the Americans who were taking their chances on Abilene. The citizens of this early building boom located their addresses a few blocks away from the tracks and the busy thrum of downtown. In 1881, Tom Hill built perhaps the town's first lumber home, a simple two room plank abode on Beech Street. An enterprising fellow, he then constructed a four room hall-and-parlor style box house—typical of the American South—just a block away at the southeast corner of Orange and North Sixth. He rented the better house to the passels of newcomers, and enjoyed this revenue until a new wife and a growing family forced him to move into the house himself.

Other families made their marks on the land as well. Elijah and Molly Watson crafted a more intricate Folk/Victorian-style domicile on about eight blocks south of Hill on Poplar Street, also on the edge of town in 1882. Just seven years later attorney Henry Sayles and his wife Hattie erected a Queen Anne style Victorian a mile further west from downtown along a wagon track that would soon bear his family name, Sayles Boulevard, and about four blocks past the original Abilene city limits. The little town on the prairie was spreading out.

Settlements, like the families that create them, age. As prosperity waxes and wanes, the kind of dwellings that go up change to reflect their fortunes. Starter homes give way to statement homes. Some houses are kept as memorials to those who once lived there, but eventually—like a grave in a country cemetery—those that remember and care no longer come along to tend the memory. They are landmarks, to be sure, but also mark the passing of lives and

An early Abilene Home

generations. Newcomers occupy the hand-me-down homes while new structures rise from the sod.

Commercial and public buildings also make a statement about economic cycles of boom and bust. Larger stores, offices, warehouses, and yards speak to the prosperity of a business; church congregations outgrow their sanctuaries and succeeding structures become architectural testaments to the popularity of that denomination's beliefs. Architects design government buildings to project the power and prestige of the rule of law, but as the population grows, so does its government. Eventually, the human occupants of most built environments outgrow their original boundaries. Structures once deemed adequate begin to decay. Space and function requirements change, and old buildings, like old clothes, are passed down to new owners or are discarded entirely.

Growing populations adjust property values as neighborhoods rise and decline. There are winners and losers in such a game. Locations once deemed desirable become a backwater as new enterprises spring up on different corners, often times businesses that reflect changes in times and conditions. Likewise with public facilities. The land retains value even as boards and windows fall apart. As a particular address increases in worth, so does the likelihood that the structure that occupies that plot will reflect wealth and prestige, often at the expense of older existing construction. Having outgrown the needs of simple utilitarian function, these second-generation structures made a statement to friends and neighbors about the importance and influence of their owners. The citizens of early Abilene who accompanied the town out of its lumber stage and into its brick era by the end of the 1800s were, in essence, the winners and stakeholders of the founding generation—or their immediate heirs. This second cohort of Abilene citizens made their own marks on the land, often covering over the traces of those that had come before.

Of course, architectural style and building materials also changed. In 1881, lumber hauled by rail was the rule. Homeowners often copied designs from pattern books or from houses they had known as kids. By 1900, though, masonry had replaced frame construction as the typical medium. Electricity came to town, too, and new structures took advantage of this power source, changing their shape and form as Abilene marked its fortieth birthday. Automobiles soon outnumbered horse-drawn conveyances, and Abilene installed an electric trolley system to carry people around town. Homes also became larger to accommodate indoor plumbing, modern appliances, and families with more leisure time on their hands. Abilene, once a rough lumber and elbow grease sort of town, transformed into a shade-tree and Sunday stroll kind of city.

As the structures of Abilene became more permanent, more solid, so did the fabric of the new town's society. The old frontier sensibilities of young men on the make gave way to more settled patterns of family life and stability as the nineteenth century faded into memory. Town leaders understood that education often sparked prosperity and in 1892 Abilene Baptist College—later Simmons College and then Hardin-Simmons University— began classes on donated land some two miles north of the tracks. A 1902 election outlawed the sale or consumption of liquor in the town, and three years later Childers Classical Institute opened, a Church of Christ college and forebear of present-day Abilene Christian University. Lytle Lake, a man-made reservoir east of town, provided a solution to the prairie town's unreliable water supply by the beginning of the twentieth century. As though confirming the wisdom and foresight of the town's founding generation, Abilene's population continued to grow, and new streets joined the old grid as the footprint of the city grew.

By the turn of the century, Abilene made a much larger mark on the landscape and boundaries of the town expanded. New streets now bore the names of famous families from the town's founding, monuments that gave ownership and meaning to Abilene's history. Houses that once lay well out in the country were now much nearer to town. Cattlemen and ranchers that had made their fortunes out on the plains now, in their prosperity, moved to town to give their families the benefits of urban civilization. Even so, they liked their space.

A few commercial buildings remain from this era, and represent a cross-section of structures that avoided the wrecking ball by luck or because they remained useful or interesting beyond their typical lifespan. Owners adapted the use of some of these survivors so that they remained relevant through time, while others languish, intact but vacant. Local philanthropists saw the merit in restoring many of these structures and retooling them for more current purposes. The continued importance of the Texas and Pacific Railroad to the city can be seen by the structures that remain near the tracks. Even the majestic county courthouse felt the bite of demolition after thirty years, to

be replaced by the more staid and businesslike 1914 Taylor County Courthouse that still stands on the site.

There were other amenities added to the town. Civic boosters purchased forty acres just southwest of town and donated them to the city as a site for an annual fair. Before long this property at the far end of Seventh Street included display buildings, a race track, and a football field and helped draw new residents to that corner of town. This space, Fair Park then, Rose Park now, became a focal point and outlet for locals with leisure time.

The decade of the 1920s was, for Abilene like much of the rest of the nation, a time of galloping prosperity. Businesses expanded on the foundations laid over the previous forty years, and the grandchildren of the pioneers expanded their holdings and influence in the city. National trends also caught up with the city, and new businesses came to town, attracted by its growing population and impressive transportation facilities. City services grew, the size and scope of neighborhoods increased, and the boundaries of the city expanded once again. Buildings once more rose and fell, the survivors communicating something of Abilene's history, but now mixed and mingled with newcomers to the landscape.

McMurry, a Methodist school, took its place as the last of the great triumvirate of Christian colleges in Abilene. Established in 1923, its first building, appropriately named Old Main, still stands as a touchstone of McMurry's founding and it still houses classrooms and offices of many of its Liberal Arts faculty. It also boasted one of the finest auditoriums in the region and hosted many city functions during the 1920s.

In recognition that most of Abilene's residents lived on the north side, city planners located the cavernous headquarters of the electric trolley system at 1021 Clinton street. The Old Car Barn, as it came to be known, started by housing streetcars riding tracks along the town's neighborhoods, eventually going as far south as McMurry College with a spur line. Nevertheless, transportation trends changed, and the building now lays abandoned and rusting, a landmark of another time and place, but still standing.

Other projects followed this trend toward the southwest. Among the new landmarks, Abilene High School opened its doors in 1924 on South First, convenient to neighborhoods on both sides of the tracks. It would later see service as Lincoln Junior High. The 1926 construction of Alta Vista Elementary school on South Eleventh marked additional city investment in the growing south side.

In the old downtown, older buildings gave way to a new wave of landmarks. The increase in automobiles led to the construction of one remnant from this era, the Rhodes Automotive Building at the corner of North First and Cedar. Other brick edifices marked the changing time, including Abilene's first skyscraper, the Alexander Building, built in 1927 at 104 Pine Street where old Abilene landmarks like the Palace Hotel had stood just a generation before. That same year, a consortium of businessmen calling themselves the Abilene Hotel Company completed an even taller landmark, this time a fourteen-story hotel in the 400 block of Pine that they leased to Conrad Hilton—the first lodging to bear his name.

These tall beacons of prosperity would soon have company on the West Texas horizon. West Texas Utilities opened an electricity generating plant, spurred by the local community's increased demand for power, that also supplied ice. Although now dormant, its massive smoke stacks still mark an important phase in the development of Abilene and were, for years, one of its most notable landmarks.

Other creations graced the landscape a little way out from downtown. Simmons College continued to thrive, while just to the south of the campus, the West Texas Baptist Sanitarium opened for business in 1924, one of the only medical facilities in the region between Fort Worth and El Paso. Childers Classical Institute, now called Abilene Christian College, relocated in 1929 from North First and Graham to land once part of the Hashknife Ranch, just northeast of downtown and east of Simmons College.

As Abilene faced its fiftieth anniversary, the decade of the 1920s seemed to indicate that prosperity had arrived. The population more than doubled, exceeding 23,000 souls. Twenty miles to the south, a new reservoir, Lake Abilene, caught water from the hills, and piped it to town to satisfy the demands of a booming population. Workers completed a third, Kirby Lake, near the decade's end and a fourth, Lake Fort Phantom, was in the works. The Bankhead Highway, America's first trans-continental motorway—then later U.S. Highway 80—came through town along South Eleventh to Oak, then north to South First Street. With it arrived some of the region's first tourists and motor court hotels as well as clusters of auto repair shops and gasoline stations along the route.

Prosperity also brought more leisure time. Car races, polo, Coach P.E. Shotwell's Abilene High School football games, and even a zoo offered a variety of entertainment options at Fair Park. Southeast of town, the Abilene Country Club opened along the banks of Cedar Creek in what was, then at least, wide-open country. Its nine-hole golf course beckoned to city dwellers who were developing a taste for a lifestyle brought about by the joys of money-making. These times of plenty, however, would not last.

The 1929 Stock Market Crash and subsequent economic depression spread a pall across the nation, and Abilene residents did their best to make due and wait for a better day coming. Now, landmarks took on a new meaning. In days past, buildings and institutions were shrines to their founders. Now they honored their saviors. The Baptist Sanitarium became Hendrick Hospital in gratitude to the Thomas Hendrick family, who also founded a Hendrick Home for Children later in the decade. Declining enrollments threatened to shutter the local colleges, but John J. Hardin put up the money to save Abilene Christian and Simmons College; the Baptist school became Hardin-Simmons University thereafter.

A few buildings went up during these hard times, but mostly as holdovers from the cash fat 1920s. Among these were the enterprises of long-time resident H.O. Wooten, including the monumental, sixteen-story, two-hundred-room Spanish art-deco Wooten Hotel, which dominates the downtown Abilene skyline to this day. In the same 300 block of Cypress Street, Wooten paid for the Paramount Theater, designing it in a complimentary Spanish revival style.

The Federal government intervened to infuse Abilene with badly needed cash by embarking upon construction projects. Near Buffalo Gap, workers from the Civilian Conservation Corps crafted a complex of red sandstone builds that would eventually serve as the nucleus of Abilene State Park. By 1936, downtown boasted of a brand new Federal Building complete with art deco details of the region's history. The biggest boost to the local economy at the hands of the American taxpayers yet came in 1940 with the creation of Camp Barkeley and, later, Tye Army Air Field. World War II brought with it a population of sixty thousand young soldiers—more than twice as many as there were residents in Abilene—just eight miles from town. With the arrival of the first trainload of khaki-clad troops, the city renewed the love affair this region has had with the military since the founding of Fort Phantom Hill. New houses went up, and new businesses opened to cater to the needs of the troops and the contractors who supported them. The end of the war may have shuttered the camp but the boom times it brought rolled on. The persistence of city leaders paid off with the establishment of Dyess Air Force Base in 1956, perhaps the greatest city landmark of all. Since that time its bombers and transport aircraft have become fixtures in the Abilene skies.

Abilene continued to grow in the 1950s. New neighborhoods like "Old Elmwood," rose up to the west along the banks of Elm Creek and swallowed up the old homesteads that once dotted the prairie. More modest homes filled in the distances between established neighborhoods and these new outliers. As Abilene's population ballooned from 23,000 in 1930 to more than 90,000 by 1960, more and more of the open spaces that had once fringed the town disappeared in a flurry of urban sprawl and industrial development. Old structures gave way to new, and places once considered important to the development of the community now felt the bite of the bulldozer's blade to make room for additional development. Interstate 20 curled its ribbon of asphalt around the northern edges of town and marked in dramatic terms one of the new boundaries of this city on the grassy plains. Other high-speed highways did similar work to the west, south, and east, until Abilene lay egg-like on

Abilene at sunset

the prairie, its distinctive oval signature filling out toward the new highways.

In 1970, the Abilene Civic Center, another landmark on the road toward the city's maturation, opened on North Sixth. It also signaled a change in architecture, ushering in the International or Modern movement to the city. For the next twenty years, building after building became monuments to this trend—a startling visual break from the conventions that that had held sway for last few decades. A new, imposing Taylor County Courthouse built in this same style opened in 1972, dwarfing the 1912 structure across the street. The following year, the Taylor County Expo center and complex continued this same style, an imposing slab sided landmark next to Shotwell Stadium and across the street from the relocated Abilene Zoo, opened six years before.

In many ways, the city and its citizens began to have a conversation of what it meant to live in this prairie city. One side enjoyed the rich heritage and legacy of the pioneers and dreamers that had come before. They cherished the architectural symbols of those by-gone days. Others, however, craved a full engagement with the future. The landmarks added to the Abilene landscape during the most recent decades have been expressions of this dialogue worked out in brick, glass, and steel.

There were new trends in the property development as well. The city that once had expanded evenly toward the north, west, and south, now grew increasingly lopsided as its new population left the old residential zones and homesteaded further south. The creation of the Mall of Abilene in 1979 helped to cement this trend and cre-

ated the impetus for a new commercial center. The old downtown faded quickly. Additional development in the 1970s through the 1990s almost always trended toward the south.

In 1984, the twenty-floor Enterprise Building at South Fifth between Chestnut and Sycamore came to dominate the skyline. Its lofty shaft stood in stark, modern contrast to the remnants of downtown just a few blocks north and across the tracks. Similarly, the creation of a large new Medical complex on the far southern edge of town marked the steady development of the city toward the hills of Buffalo Gap and away from the traditional centers of wealth, real estate value, and business. The rise of oil barons in the 1970s fueled the rise of these new monuments, including a new country club for a new generation, Fairway Oaks.

A massive intervention of philanthropic and economic development dollars saved downtown from the crushing grip and a decades-old cycle of decay. With this process arrested, Abilene struggled again to achieve some kinds of development equilibrium. Landmarks of previous years, fallen on hard times and neglect, emerged afresh in a variety of new functions, housing everything from city bureaus to arts and heritage organizations. This adaptive use of existing structures championed by such organizations as Preserve America and the National Trust for Historic Preservation found a willing laboratory in Abilene.

At the same time, the shiny glass and steel office of the new oil-soaked era fell hard against the immutable laws of economics. When the boom turned to bust in the 1980s, even these nouveau landmarks fell prey. In one novel turnabout and example of latter-day adaptive use, the sleek 1970s headquarters of a fast living oil concern became home to a more traditional Abilene use: Wylie United Methodist Church.

Now, as times change, Abilene no longer serves as the great warehouse and shipping center it had been in its earliest days. Instead, it has become the commercial, banking, education, medical, and retail hub of a large swath of West Texas, and the city image and development dialogue has shifted directions yet again. The emergence of the Wal-Mart Supercenter complex on the northeast edge of town in 2005 promises to move development in that direction, once again away from the traditional centers downtown, but also away from the commercial and residential sprawl of the south side.

In the end, perhaps the high-tech addition of Frontier Texas is the most symbolic of the Abilene landmarks. It is a facility of studied and deliberate architectural contrasts. The story this modern museum tells is ancient—in essence the genesis story of West Texas—but its techniques involve a wide variety of futuristic gadgetry. At the same time,

Frontier Texas makes a bold new architectural statement in Abilene, while at the same time relying on old landmarks to make its point. In that educational center—designed to pass on to rising generations the story of who they are—the building itself points the way across the bewildering and complex story of this prairie town.

There, just to the west, stand faux chimneys.

Just like those of at Fort Phantom Hill from a hundred and fifty years ago.

Just like the original marks on the land.

Abilene spreads out all around, a sprawling of the new and shiny, the old and regal, and the spent and aging. To an outsider unfamiliar with life on the prairie, Abilene is something of an acquired aesthetic. Even so, the wide, bright skies and the nearly boundless horizons that frame the decades of landmarks that illustrate every twist and turn of the city's history continue to create a place inviting to visitors and newcomers alike. Abilene's is an American story.

In the end, Abilene yields an intangible magnificence composed of all its landmarks, all its history, and all of its people.

The chimneys of Fort Phantom Hill

B-1 bomber over Abilene

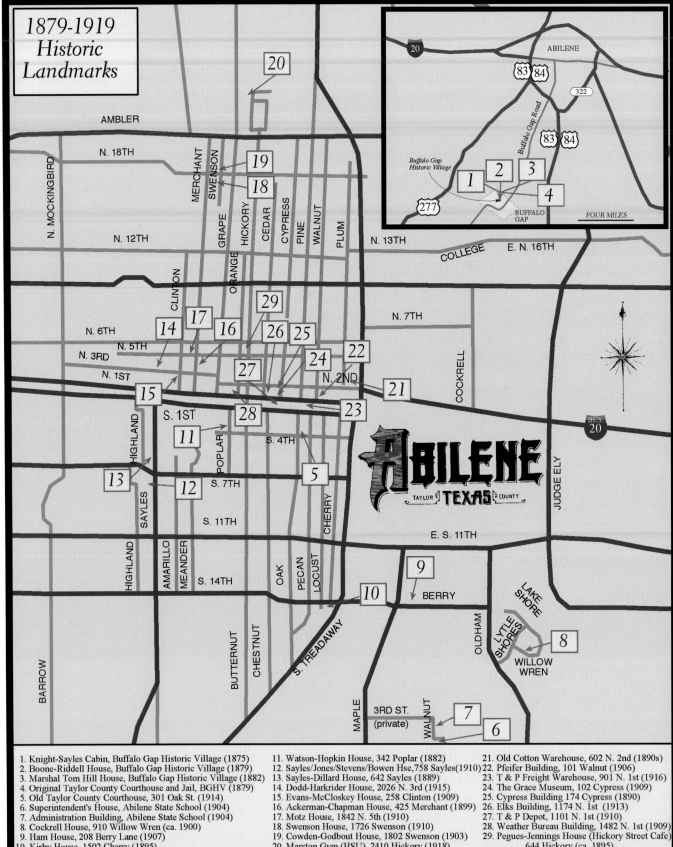

1879-1919 Historic Landmarks

26

1. Knight-Sayles Cabin, Buffalo Gap Historic Village (1875)
2. Boone-Riddell House, Buffalo Gap Historic Village (1879)
3. Marshal Tom Hill House, Buffalo Gap Historic Village (1882)
4. Original Taylor County Courthouse and Jail, BGHV (1879)
5. Old Taylor County Courthouse, 301 Oak St. (1914)
6. Superintendent's House, Abilene State School (1904)
7. Administration Building, Abilene State School (1904)
8. Cockrell House, 910 Willow Wren (ca. 1900)
9. Ham House, 208 Berry Lane (1907)
10. Kirby House, 1502 Cherry (1895)

11. Watson-Hopkin House, 342 Poplar (1882)
12. Sayles/Jones/Stevens/Bowen Hse, 758 Sayles(1910)
13. Sayles-Dillard House, 642 Sayles (1889)
14. Dodd-Harkrider House, 2026 N. 3rd (1915)
15. Evans-McCloskey House, 258 Clinton (1909)
16. Ackerman-Chapman House, 425 Merchant (1899)
17. Motz House, 1842 N. 5th (1910)
18. Swenson House, 1726 Swenson (1910)
19. Cowden-Godbout House, 1802 Swenson (1903)
20. Marston Gym (HSU), 2410 Hickory (1918)

21. Old Cotton Warehouse, 602 N. 2nd (1890s)
22. Pfeifer Building, 101 Walnut (1906)
23. T & P Freight Warehouse, 901 N. 1st (1916)
24. The Grace Museum, 102 Cypress (1909)
25. Cypress Building 174 Cypress (1890)
26. Elks Building, 1174 N. 1st (1913)
27. T & P Depot, 1101 N. 1st (1910)
28. Weather Bureau Building, 1482 N. 1st (1909)
29. Pegues-Jennings House (Hickory Street Cafe) 644 Hickory (ca. 1895)

1875–1919

To understand Abilene, perhaps it is best to start with Buffalo Gap, the great nursery of the present city. After all, its courthouse and tree-shaded lots were the first West Texas homes of many of the pioneering families who first settled this country. When the Texas and Pacific cut the prairie a few hours' ride to the north, many of Buffalo Gap's more ambitious residents headed that direction, leaving the little settlement in the hills behind to make their futures along the gleaming rails of progress.

The buildings on this tour represent the founding era of Abilene, a time that began with hard-working people building simple homes and businesses along the tracks but ending with all the makings of a respectable town. Before long, impressive brick structures graced downtown, two church-affiliated colleges had put down roots, and the highly touted "Future Great City of West Texas" appeared well on its way to fulfilling that prophecy.

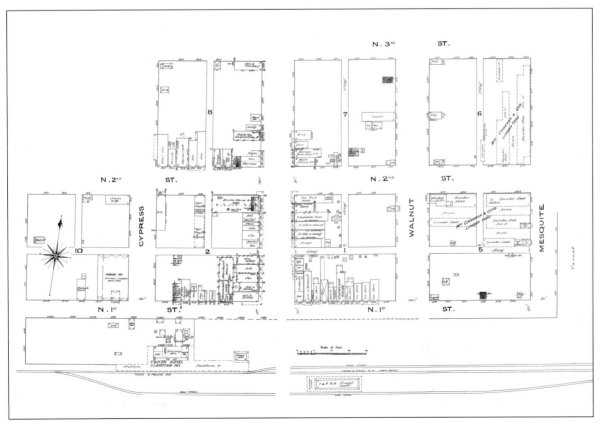

A portion of the Sanborn Fire Insurance map for Abilene, 1885, showing businesses spreading out along North First and Pine.

Buffalo Gap Historic Village

by Donald S. Frazier

J.M.C. Knight was hunting buffalo when he first saw the country that is now Taylor County. Born in South Carolina in 1821, he had started moving west before the Civil War, settling in eastern Alabama. After the war, he moved on to western Arkansas, then to San Saba County, Texas. A farmer with a growing family—his wife Susannah would eventually bear him fifteen children, ten of whom lived past infancy—he was constantly looking for other opportunities to earn some money. In 1875, after trying his hand at commercial hunting and apparently making enough to buy land, he moved his family, including the six youngest children, to a scenic part of Elm Creek west of Buffalo Gap. This cabin was the Knight home. From this humble abode, typical of southern single-pen log cabin, the family raised cattle, bought more land, and prospered.

After Susannah died in 1897, and J.M.C. the following year, one of the Knight children sold the old home place to Henry Sayles, an attorney and one of the founders of Abilene. His son, Henry Sayles, Jr., an oil man, rancher, and real estate developer, acquired the property in 1916 and sold it the next year to the city for the construction of Lake Abilene. He relocated the old log cabin first to another part of his ranch, then into town as a promotional attraction for the Elmwood housing development. He eventually moved the increasingly dilapidated cabin back to his ranch before giving it to Ernie Wilson in 1956 for use in his Old West Museum.

Buffalo Gap Historic Village

by Donald S. Frazier

Tradition has it that an obedient husband agreed to urgings of his persistent and persuasive spouse to build this house. The story goes that she, much younger than he, had followed him to the Texas frontier in the middle of the 1870s where he ran a cattle operation around Bluff Creek near present-day Winters. Their home, according to legend, was a tree house in a large oak tree. There, she would prepare food for the cowboys, then lower the meals down in a bucket. There would be no mingling between the pretty young wife and the scruffy saddle tramps!

When children came to the couple, she insisted that they have a proper home, and not a hut among the branches. She wanted to move to town—which in 1879 meant Buffalo Gap. Convinced, the cowman bought plans and contracted with carpenters to raise the original part of this four-room structure just a block away from the new county courthouse. A great example of Gothic Revival architecture, this house is almost identical to the Dwight D. Eisenhower birthplace in Denison, Texas, now administered by the Texas Historical Commission for public use.

This home predates the city of Abilene by two years and is perhaps the oldest family residence still standing at its original site in the county. Additions in the early twentieth century and others in the 1960s have changed the appearance and floor plan of the back of the house, but the original lines remain intact. It is now part of the Texas Frontier Heritage and Cultural Center which plans to restore the house and open it to overnight visitors.

Buffalo Gap Historic Village

by Catherine K. Pace

Tom Hill, Marshal of Abilene, built two houses on the north side of the town in 1882. The first, he constructed to live in, and the second he built as a rental property. The house standing today at the Buffalo Gap Historic Village was originally this rent house, which stood at the southeast corner of North Sixth and Orange Streets.

Hill built the house with the standard "shotgun-style" frame. The phrase "shotgun-style" describes any house with rooms built in a line, with no way into the inner rooms, apart from through the outer ones. The term "shotgun" refers to the idea that, with all the doors open, a person could fire a shotgun all the way through from front to back. The three rooms on the left-hand side of the house are the original 1882 part of the structure.

Although Hill initially built the house to rent out, in 1885, his growing family had to move in because it was larger than their other home. Hill added onto the house in preparation for the family to move in. The addition included the following: the hall-way, the parlor on the right side of the building, a back porch, and a storage room. Basically, the renovated house looked much like it does today.

At only thirty-two years of age, Marshal Tom Hill died in an accidental shooting in 1886. After his death, his wife Mollie had to raise their daughter Belle in this house. Neither woman worked outside the home, and they had trouble making ends meet. The women made greeting cards that they sold door-to-door and to local merchants. Even so, they could not afford to keep the house repaired and even had to resort to covering the walls with newspaper to attempt to keep out the harsh winter winds.

After an incredibly hard life, Mollie Hill died in 1952 at the age of ninety-eight, and Belle, who never married, stayed with her through thick and thin, through hunger and cold, dying only eight years later in 1960, at the age of seventy-six. The house moved to the Ernie Wilson Museum of the Old West in 1964, the predecessor to the Buffalo Gap Historic Village.

Buffalo Gap Historic Village

by Catherine K. Pace

In 1879, the citizens of Taylor County began construction on their first courthouse in Buffalo Gap, the county seat. Workers completed the two-story square structure in March 1880, making it the largest building in the community. It was built from local stone, and masons placed cannonballs in carved-out hollows in between the layers. Will Masters, a local builder, hauled the cannonballs by ox-drawn wagon from Vicksburg, Mississippi.

Downstairs were the courtroom and offices for the judge, sheriff, and the county attorney. The upstairs, however, was quarters for criminals. The larger room had twelve bunk beds for those who committed petty crimes. The small solitary cell at the top of the stairs, however, was reserved for criminals who had committed more serious and violent crimes.

The 1883 election that moved the county seat thirteen miles north to Abilene meant that further hopes of expanding or replacing the courthouse in Buffalo Gap were abandoned. Instead, Abilene citizens made plans to place the new one near the Texas and Pacific Railroad tracks on Chestnut Street in their city.

The county used the jail in Buffalo Gap for a few years, but eventually sold the structure to private owners. The new owners converted the building into a residential duplex. In 1956, Ernie Wilson bought the property and turned it into the "Ernie Wilson Museum of the Old West." The original Taylor County Courthouse and Jail is now a part of the Buffalo Gap Historic Village and is available to the public.

This photograph from the 1970s shows the original Taylor County Courthouse serving as an Old West museum. The J.M.C. Knight log cabin sits just beyond the building. Originally, the courthouse had one door on the front, a rectangular window above it, and arched windows on the ground floor. After the county seat moved to Abilene, this building sold to private citizens who modified it for use as a home. Notice the upstairs window to the right. The owners created it by taking the much smaller slit windows (the opening seen in the middle allowed in air and light, but was originally secured by two rows of metal bars) on the second story and enlarging them to match the window to the left. The result was, structurally, far from satisfactory. The seam between two of the building stones above lies unsupported over the new opening, leading to a crack in the masonry, and the bottom sill is shorter than its counterpart to the left. On the ground floor, residents crafted a door from one of the original windows to create a duplex home. The original roof may have been flat with a stone parapet.

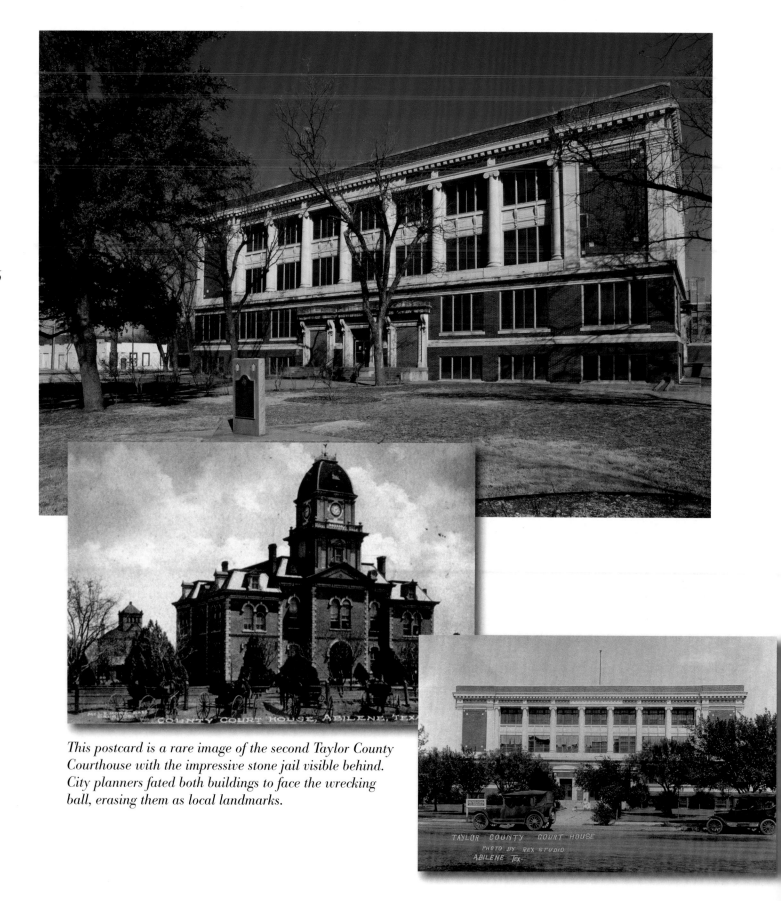

36

This postcard is a rare image of the second Taylor County Courthouse with the impressive stone jail visible behind. City planners fated both buildings to face the wrecking ball, erasing them as local landmarks.

301 Oak Street

by Tiffany Lynn Grove

Reflecting the progress Abilene had made as a city moving into the second decade of the 20th century, citizens voted in 1913 to build a courthouse with a classic Revival style to represent Taylor County. This would be the third permanent structure to serve as the seat of the county government. Abilene residents viewed the previous courthouse, built in 1884 as not only out-dated but also as unsafe. The newer three-story brick courthouse would be second one located at 300 Oak Street.

In February 1913, many residents petitioned the commissioner's court to build a new courthouse. As a result, the commissioners made a special committee to inspect the edifice. Following the committee's examination of the building, they agreed with the petitioners that the current courthouse was unsafe, and on March 29, 1913, a bond issue with a budget of $150,000, passed with a vote of 1,282 to 769.

After careful consideration of four Texas architectural firms, the county commissioners voted to have George Burnett of Waco build the courthouse. He applied his classic Revival design to a three-story, flat-roofed rectangular building. The commissioners chose contractor A. Z. Rogers, who had the lowest bid of $119,785 and even lowered it later to $117,900, to build this Taylor County landmark. In order to make way for the new courthouse, the county had C. A. Clayton demolish the 1884 version. During the sixteen-month construction project, county offices were temporarily held on the first floor of the Grace Hotel. For renting four rooms, the county paid the hotel $80 per month. Finally, on May 17, 1915, the builders finished.

In 1954, the courthouse underwent several renovations. Besides remodeling each floor, the county also installed air conditioning. However, all of the remodeling did not meet the needs of a growing Abilene. By November 1966, Abilenians realized that Taylor County needed a newer courthouse. Once again, the residents petitioned for a more modern building. The commissioners created the Committee of One Hundred to analyze the structure. The team stated that the edifice was safe but behind "in the light of modern day office practices and methods." Although they commended the "visionary judgment" of its builders, a larger, updated form was necessary. In the summer of 1972, the county government moved once again, but this time across the street to the current Taylor County Courthouse. The columned building became known as the Old Taylor County Courthouse while the present one is known simply as the Taylor County Courthouse.

Abilene State School

by Kensey Robert Allen

In 1897 Texas State Governor Joseph D. Sayers appointed a commission of experienced men to select a site for a State Epileptic Hospital—termed an Epileptic Colony. Local Abilene residents hoped that the state would build the colony in Abilene to boost the local economy. Henry A. Tillet, a state senator from Abilene, realized his city was not in the running due to its lack of water supply, so he organized an effort to overcome this problem. A group of citizens helped the city purchase the land and build Lytle Lake. As a result the legislature named Abilene the site of the Epileptic Colony, which opened its doors on March 26, 1904.

At the beginning patients received care for $5.00 a week. Even at such a bargain, the facility was close to being self-sufficient. Residents ran a livestock operation as well as tending to fruit orchards. In 1925 the facility became Abilene State Hospital, and in 1957, after changing its role to caring for the mentally retarded and impaired, it was designated the Abilene State School.

One of the original buildings at the school was the Superintendent's House, which is still standing today. Architect William Proctor Preston designed the house, which was one of four buildings constructed at the site in 1904. The beautiful 6,500-square-foot home cost $7300. The brick façade with white trim demonstrates a classic Colonial Revival influence. It has a covered back porch, which, during the heyday of the Epileptic Colony, gave views of nothing but open country. The school was quite far away from the city. Dr. John Preston was the first occupant of the house as well as the first superintendent of the facility. Perhaps the most famous superintendent to occupy the house was Dr. T. B. Bass, renowned for his research in epilepsy. Some of his earliest research even involved using rattlesnake venom to treat residents, and also Dr. Bass believed that treatment should include proper diet, light work, and regular working and sleeping hours. Every superintendent and his family received free room and board until 2001, when the state began to charge state housing fees based on square footage. This action made the home unaffordable as a residence.

The house is beautiful on the interior. It has spacious luxurious rooms with giant windows, and little nooks and crannies for storage. The home consists of two stories and has three bedrooms upstairs and five rooms downstairs. Today the house has been restored to its original luster, mostly to the credit of Rick and Jayma Savage, who lived in the house while Rick was an associate to the superintendent. They saw the potential of the old home and took on the task of restoring it to its glory days. The building still provides some of the most interesting architecture seen in Abilene.

Abilene State School

by Kensey Robert Allen

The Old Administration Building on the campus of Abilene State School has remained a fixture in the landscape of the facility since its construction began in 1901. Abilene citizens donated $3,200 so the city could purchase 640 acre of land from Judge Fred Cockrell and J.G. Lowden. The land was then given to the state for a state hospital for people with epilepsy. The committee hired by Governor Joseph Sayers selected the Abilene location stating, "it is by far the most suitable for asylum purposes." The final overall cost of construction of the facility amounted for $200,000, which equaled four- fifths of the capital stock in the three banks in Abilene at the time. When the facility opened the citizens viewed some of the finest state buildings in Texas outside the state's capital. The patients were responsible for many of the everyday operations of the school.

Construction on the Administration building ended in 1904. It was the center of everything that went on in the facility. It also served as the front of the campus. Like the Superintendent's House a few hundred yards away, the Old Administration Building is one of four original structures remaining today. It is made of red brick and has a classic Federal style design. It has three stories, two above ground and one below. The front facing of the building has a white Roman-style entrance with four Doric columns leading up to the three main entrances. The steps leading to the entrances are made of sandstone with each step eight inches thick. The building housed the Superintendent's office, handled all the patients documents, as well as all the business dealings that went on with the facility. Also on the first floor there is a beautiful original vault. The vault still has a painting of the Epileptic Hospital from which today's institution grew, and the vault window can still be seen from outside the facility by locating the steel and riveted window just to the south of the back entrance. The building has gradually begun to lose its importance as the school continues to grow and upgrade. It is currently being used as an office for a state architect.

The presence of the Epileptic Hospital and its successor, the Abilene State School, has always been a major contributor to the economy of Abilene. At the time of it original construction, the site quickly became the city's leading employer. Even today, with the influx of multiple major industries in Abilene, the state school remains the fifth largest-employer in Abilene. The Old Administration Building is a true landmark of this success.

910 Willow Wren

by Josiah Allen

The two story structure at 910 Willow Wren helps to tell an important part of the history of Abilene from the turn of the twentieth century.

Judge Fred Cockrell, who built the home, was influential in the early stages of Abilene's development. He was one of the major proponents of building Lytle Lake in 1897 to secure a more stable water supply for Abilene. Part of his motivation was to win over the legislature in their decision to place a state hospital for epileptics. This endeavor was successful, and the State Epileptic Hospital came to Abilene a few years later. The site later became the Abilene State School. Cockrell was also quite an important catalyst in helping start Abilene's first water company.

The house at 910 Willow Wren is intimately connected to Lytle Lake in many ways. Not only was its original owner responsible for the lake, stonemasons crafted this home from large stones excavated during the digging of the dam for the lake. The solid stone structure, which is located just to the west of Lytle Lake, has required very little renovation in more than a century since its construction. The Cockrell House, like Abilene, has stood the test of time.

208 Berry Lane

by Leah Herod

The farmhouse at 208 Berry Lane is an important reminder of the way that Abilene was at the beginning of the twentieth century. Once located in the country, this farmhouse is one of Abilene's oldest remaining houses. The home is situated on a hill overlooking the valley of Cedar Creek to the west. Once unpopulated, the once scenic valley is now dominated by South Treadway Boulevard, railroad tracks, and commercial development. Berry Lane was much more secluded in the early 1900s as well. The Kirby House at the end of Cherry Street on a nearby hill west of Cedar Creek was the closest neighbor.

The story starts with an entrepreneur named Zack Taylor Adams. Originally from Alabama, Adams came to Texas on horseback following the Civil War. He ran a candy store in Weatherford, where he married Ida Kindel in 1887. They moved to Abilene in 1890. Adams became a pioneer in the Abilene grocery business, operating several stores, including one at North Third and Pine.

In 1907 Adams built the two-story farmhouse on Berry Lane where he and Ida reared four children. Adams's structure is a good example of a Vernacular Folk farmhouse. It is a wooden, two-story, white house with a porch that wraps all the way around the dwelling. The house is spacious, having four bedrooms upstairs and one downstairs. There is also a large kitchen, den, and dining room.

The Adams house features hardwood floors, along with a beautiful but simple wooden staircase visible as soon as one enters the front door. The woodwork in the house is in a style known as bull's-eye—where the trim meets at the top of the walls and is decorated with wood that gives it the appearance of a target or bull's-eye. This feature is only on the first floor because it would have been much more expensive for the Adams family to decorate the entire house in this style. Two fireplaces that share a chimney warm the house.

The Adamses enjoyed living in the country for almost a decade until two disasters uprooted them. Adams's grocery businesses were destroyed between Abilene's flood of July 13, 1911, and the downtown fire on August 15, 1911. In 1915 they left Abilene and moved north to Lubbock, Texas.

After a long period without occupants in the house, R.P. and Beth Ham moved to the residence in the 1960s. The house has changed little in appearance over the years with continued preservation. The white farmhouse has never seen another color and the hardwood floors are the original. Although built with no bathrooms, the Hams added one on the first and second floor. This expansion changed the layout of the house and cut into part of the back porch. Nevertheless, while Abilene continues to change, the old farmhouse truly takes you back in time.

1502 Cherry Street

by Catherine Ann Watjen

In just a little over a decade after Abilene's founding, the fledgling city had grown significantly. Houses, business, and other structures arose along both sides of the Texas and Pacific Railroad tracks. Fourteen blocks south of the tracks, however, was still relatively open prairie land. It was here, at 1502 Cherry Street, that E.N. Kirby built his house in 1895.

Kirby was born in La Grange, Georgia, in 1865. In 1892, at the age of 27, he made the brave move to Abilene, which was then a struggling new West Texas town. For the next fifty-five years, Kirby was one of Abilene's most respected attorneys. He also served as mayor of the city for thirteen years. Kirby died in 1949, but his legacy lives on. His family donated land to the city that would eventually bear the names Kirby Lake and Kirby Park, both honoring this Abilene pioneer.

Although the Kirby House still has its original layout, many renovations and additions have been made to this Victorian-style home. Its steep roof with some sharp angles and ornate porch are just some classical examples of what it is to be Victorian. Tragically, a fire broke out in the upper levels of the home in 1949. The damages were soon repaired and the home remains remarkably intact. Four years later servant's quarters were added. As a growing trend along many other houses across the nation, the owners added a pool to the property in 1959. With progress comes change. The Kirby House has kept watch for more than a century from this location and has adapted with time. It stands as a wonderful reminder of the early days of Abilene and people who built it.

342 Poplar Street

by Kensey Robert Allen

One year after Abilene's founding in 1881, Elijah W. Watson built his family home on Poplar Street, just three blocks south of the Texas and Pacific Railroad tracks. Now known as the Watson-Hopkin House, the structure is one of the oldest single-family homes in Abilene. The one-and-a-half story frame cottage is in the architectural style of a Victorian folk home with some Queen Anne style features, such as the two dormers with the fish-scale wood pattern that were popular among homes of this particular style. The building features a pitched roof supported on the front with four simple columns. It also boasts an attached covered porch with two big windows flanking the large front door.

The original owners of the house were Elijah and Molly Watson. Elijah had come to Texas from Tennessee and was involved in the grocery business and later came to own a transfer line. His wife Molly, her maiden name Molly E. Bell, was the granddaughter of Zachary Taylor, the twelfth president of the United States. She kept a large picture of her famed grandfather in the home for some time. The couple raised ten children in the household. Their son Will, known as "sheriff," was born in the house, and was long associated with the West Texas Fair, the Hardin–Simmons University Cowboy Band, and rode one of the HSU six white horses. Beulah Watson lived in the home many years and worked at Campbell's Department Store. Cress Watson was a volunteer fireman for years. Originally, the house had two rooms upstairs and two downstairs, with a detached kitchen. Later, a kitchen and bath were added to the house. The Watson family occupied the house from 1882 to 1929, and it is currently owned by Mac Hopkin. The house serves as a reminder of the city may have looked liked shortly after its founding.

758 Sayles Boulevard

by Joseph Trey Cox, III

The majestic Sayles/Jones/Stevens/Bowen House is tucked away behind the trees on the corner of South Seventh and Sayles Boulevard. This classical revival house was built in 1910 by Henry Sayles and is part of the Sayles Boulevard Historic District. The southwestern edge of Abilene, encompassing much of the Sayles Boulevard Historic District, was started by Henry Sayles in the 1920s. The property itself has been changed multiple times throughout history to keep up with changing technology, but the owners have been sensitive to the uniqueness of the building.

When Abilene was established in 1881, the entirety of the town was 175 city blocks, which included smaller blocks towards the core of the city and larger ones on the outskirts of town. A few prominent individuals acquired property on the outskirts of Abilene. Henry Sayles, Sr., was an attorney who acquired a hefty amount of land on the western edge of Abilene, south of the T&P railroad, which encompasses much of the Sayles Boulevard Historic District. The district stretches from South Tenth to South Fifth and from Highland to Meander. Sayles Boulevard is a street with a landscaped esplanade, which divides the flow of traffic along the thoroughfare. In addition to the Sayles/Jones/Stevens/Bowen House, Sayles Boulevard also boasts Henry Sayles 1889 house just down the street.

The Sayles/Jones/Stevens/Bowen House is an example of Greek Revival architecture. The front entrance is graced with sidelights and transoms with beveled glazing. The house is 7,390 square feet and sits on 3.2 acres on Sayles Drive. This house is a delightful landmark in the community.

51

642 Sayles Boulevard
by KC Walters

A quaint Queen Anne Victorian style home sits at the corner of Sayles and South Seventh as a testament to the times when Abilene was first created. Henry and Hattie Sayles, a prominent Abilene family for whom Sayles Boulevard is named, built the house in 1889. Henry Sayles, an attorney, hired R.W. Miller and Samuel Calvin Wagner to build his home on what was then known as Boulevard Street. The house stayed in the Sayles family until 1974, when it was sold to the Dillards. While the house looks elegant and quaint by today's standards, it was a grand house that graced the outskirts of town, away from the hustle and bustle of the newly forming city of Abilene.

The house itself features six windowed gables and dormers decorated in various patterns of cut shingles and grid pattern of half inch molding. It originally had three fireplaces located in the kitchen, master bedroom, and living room. The first floor has tall ceilings and large windows for light and airflow. Shortly after the house was built, a rear portion was added to accommodate more children. This added two additional bedrooms, a new kitchen, and laundry area.

There were also several other minor additions, including closing in a porch, turning a bedroom into a bathroom, moving the kitchen, removal of one of the fireplaces, and an exterior stairway to the second floor. The bedroom that was turned into a bathroom held the first inside toilet in the house. In 1941, a large fire did considerable damage to the second floor and the southwest portions of the house. Also the added portion of the house was enclosed to be a 'self-contained apartment.'

The Sayles family continued to grow, forcing them to build a larger home elsewhere. After the family moved, their son, John Sayles, lived in the original Sayles home with his wife and children until his death. The house was then in the possession of John's son, Jack, and the house was vacant for five years until he sold the house to Mr. and Mrs. Richard Dillard in 1974. The Dillards began an extensive restoration project on the house to return it to its original grandeur. All in all, Henry and Hattie Sayles did a number of services to the Abilene community, including leaving the jewel of a house behind for the rest of Abilene to enjoy as a glimpse into the past.

2026 North Third Street

by Edward Francis De Clements, Jr.

Coming to Abilene was still a real frontier experience at the turn of the 20th century. Ranching and the railroad were the two prominent sources of revenue. Despite the rough and dusty landscape, Abilene was starting to transition from a town to a booming city. The Dodd-Harkrider house is one of many examples of this transition.

Elizabeth Dodd had a first-hand experience with Abilene's growth when she purchased an undeveloped plot of land in 1910. Five years later, she built a typical two-story American Four-Square dwelling on the lot. This wood structure features simple lines, but was a popularly published style in magazines of the time. After living the house for only four years, she sold it to Rupert and Mary Harkrider.

The Harkriders owned the house from 1919 to 1958. Rupert worked at J.M. Radford Grocery Company. His dedication to the company allowed for several promotions—eventually to vice-president of the firm. Rupert helped the company expand to twenty-three cities in Texas and New Mexico. Mary Harkrider was not your typical stay-at-home wife. She was heavily involved in their cattle business, so much so that she became Secretary/Treasurer of the West Texas Hereford Association. Mary also initiated the local Red Cross during World War II.

The Harkrider House, as it came to be called, was sold in 1958 to Durward and Mary Grubb, teachers at Lincoln Junior High School and Abilene High School. In 1978, Michael and Mary Stedham, counselors at the First Baptist Church's Ministry of Counseling and Enrichment, bought the house. They sold the home to the current owners Donald and Lora Christensen in 1981. The Christensens have seemed to follow suit in community service and involvement. Donald is an engineer for Halliburton Logging Service, President of the Society of Professional Well Log Analysts, and a Boy Scout Leader. Lora Lynn has served as president of Harmony Club and the Abilene Music Leaders Association, and she has also served as a member of the Abilene School Board. In addition, Lora teaches private piano lessons from her home—as a result, hundreds of children have learned to play the piano in this house over the past quarter century.

Since its construction by Elizabeth Dodd, the Harkrider House has seemed to foster some type of community growth. Not only did the building itself contribute to the rural expansion of Abilene, the owners have also had a direct influence on the community.

258 Clinton Street

by Catherine Ann Watjen

A man's home is his castle. John W. Evans, the original owner of the Evans-McClosky house, built his castle at 258 Clinton Street in 1909. A rancher, farmer, grocer, husband, and father, Evans and his wife raised twelve children while maintaining their business on Pine Street. Despite this busy schedule, they were able to bring up children of great character and service. Two of his daughters went on to become local school teachers and to write textbooks for the state of Texas. The legacy of John and his family, like so many others, define who Abilenians really are.

Queen Anne herself could not have picked a prettier place to call home. Queen Anne styling, although sometimes lavish, also has many other features that define it. Queen Anne styled homes were popular in the United States in the 1880s and '90s. The Evans-McCloskey house has a simple, but classic look to it. The two-story home is vernacular in form and has a steeply pyramidal roof. This home, like so many homes built at this time, was constructed without any electricity or running water. It was not until 1919 that the owners added wiring and plumbing. Space heaters also replaced the original coal stoves. The frontal view of the home is a one story porch, which has wooden posts, a repaired balustrade, and jigsaw brackets, which give it further detailing. The porch has been completely repaired numerous times by the current owner Carrie Blaschke, who has dedicated much of her time to the renovation of this home. From its steep roof to its expansive porch, this residence will never lose its classic look.

425 Merchant Street

by Ben Newland

This quaint little house located on Merchant Street was constructed in 1899, making it one of the older residential buildings in Abilene. The original owner was Gus Ackerman, a local businessman, bookkeeper, and father to three daughters. Ackerman purchased the house in 1899 for $2,125. Currently, the house is home to Hazel Chapman, an active member of the Abilene community. Before retirement, Chapman was the owner and operator of Hazel's House of Fine Junk, a local antiques dealership.

The house is a Victorian-inspired structure, featuring the classic Victorian peaks of the roof alongside a dwarfed Victorian tower. The façade of the house is the typical columned and covered porch. Additionally, the outside surface of the structure is the wood siding featured in the majority of these homes. The paint is monochromatic in order to contrast with the sparse brick as well as the black roofing, thus accentuating the roof line. The house is a one and a half story affair with twelve-foot downstairs ceilings and short dormer ceilings in the upstairs area. One of the oldest homes in Abilene, the Ackerman-Chapman House reminds us of an earlier age.

1842 North Fifth Street

by Mandy Elson

What kind of house has two front doors, an outdoor kitchen, and no central plumbing system? The answer to this profound question is: the Motz House located at 1842 North Fifth Street in Abilene, Texas. It stands in one of Abilene's older and more intact residential neighborhoods surrounded by many contemporary buildings. The Motz House has enriched the city of Abilene through its unique architectural design.

Charles Motz was a prominent businessman dealing in real estate and insurance in the early years of Abilene, Texas. He married and had two daughters who resided in the home after the couple passed away.

Motz built the home in 1910. It is a two-story Colonial-Revival-style house that is famous for its "gambrel-style" roof. Colonial-Revival style was a popular American house style that first appeared in 1876 at the United States Centennial Exposition. The style reflects American patriotism and a desire for simplicity. Colonial-Revival houses attained only marginal popularity throughout early twentieth century Texas, and relatively few were built in Abilene.

Many features of Colonial-Revival style appear in the Motz House. The house has two stories with the entertaining rooms on the first floor with bedrooms on the upper floor. The rectangular house with a symmetrical façade has a "temple-like" entrance. The "gambrel-style" roof is rarely seen on local residential structures in Abilene. This particular roof has two slopes with a steeper lower slope and a flatter upper one. The roof had asphalt composition shingles and the exterior walls had wood siding. Along with the main house, there is a smaller dwelling to the right of the house that was used for servant's quarters. In front of the house lies a fish pond lined with the original brick work. Because of these many details, the Motz house is indeed one of Abilene's treasured landmarks.

1726 Swenson Street

by Carlos V. Montez

There was once a great Swedish migration to West Texas. One of the key figures in this movement was W.G. Swenson. It is clear that while Swenson may have been born Swedish, once he settled in Abilene, he was all Texan. Living here since the age of two, Swenson would eventually become one of the city's most important entrepreneurs and cultural pioneer.

W.G. Swenson was influential in Abilene's early commerce and infrastructure. As a child he saw the development of the tent village of Abilene into a bustling town of budding enterprises. Swenson engaged in various enterprises—banking, utilities, railroading, residential and commercial real estate, and the ice manufacturing business. Swenson married Shirley McCollum, and they had four children—two girls and two boys.

He built his family home in 1910 at the corner of North Eighteenth and Swenson. The house was one of Abilene's largest and finest residences, containing 5,800 square feet of living space that included four bedrooms and three baths. It was designed by Swenson and architect W.P. Preston. It is of the Prairie Style-Spanish Mission Revival on the exterior combined with a gracious classical Roman-Greek revival interior. The house is situated on one entire city block and is listed on the National Register of Historic Places.

The house is important because of its superb detailing, grand open interior spaces, site layout, and expertly detailed woodcraft. All of these characteristics were common in grand homes in this area during the early twentieth century. Some of most eye-catching features of the Swenson home are its stained glass windows, the entry gallery's skylight, and the finely crafted brass hardware found throughout the house.

The Swenson House's theme during 1920s was renovation—and lots of it. Then, Swenson added brick and Leuders limestone to the outside. The general shape has withstood the test of time, and the majority of it has stayed the same. During these same renovations, Swenson removed the roof's wood shake and installed clay tile in its place. This same clay tile is still in place and in excellent condition. The family replaced the wooden columns on the front of the home with arched brick columns. In order to conserve materials, they did not throw away the original wood pillars. Instead, they used them in the landscaping on the south side of the house to help support the budding grape arbor. Much of the landscaping is of natural vegetation and is drought resistant, especially useful given the unpredictable West Texas weather.

W.G. Swenson contributions to early Abilene's growth, and his home, give testament to his life and cultural. Through careful diligence and planning, the Swenson House is still an Abilene modern classical home. Now under the careful watch of the Abilene Preservation League, the home will benefit the people of Abilene for years to come.

1802 Swenson Street

by Emily Young

At the beginning of the twentieth century, people ordered many things from the Sears-Roebuck Catalog, including kitchen appliances, books, tools, clothes, furniture, dishes, toys, and houses.

Yes, houses.

C.W. Cowden built the home at 1802 Swenson from a kit he ordered from the Sears-Roebuck Catalog in 1903. He built it as a residence for his children while they attended nearby Simmons College. This house symbolizes an interesting and colorful past in Abilene, Texas.

In 1895 Sears entered the home building business. It was one of the top sellers of house plans and house supplies. After C.W. Cowden placed the order for his home Sears shipped thirty thousand pieces to the closest railroad station, with this came a seventy-five-page leather bound instruction manual. The book gave a quick piece of advice: "Do not take anyone's advice on how to assemble this building." Not all of the materials were included—no paint, varnish, roof shingles, or plaster for the walls. It did, however, give a detailed list of the materials that would be needed to complete the house.

With the children long graduated from college, the Cowdens sold the house in the 1920s to the state to serve as an orphanage. Over the next several years homeless children found refuge in its walls. Back in private hands today, the house still remains a strong reminder of early twentieth century ingenuity.

#20 Marston Gym, Hardin–Simmons University (1918)

2410 Hickory Street

by Terann Brooke Ragland

Marston Gym was completed and dedicated on the campus of Simmons College in 1918. In contrast to the masses of wooden buildings during the time period, Marston was a brick structure that took its name from the project's biggest donor, Edgar Marston. Including the balcony seating, the structure has three stories. The upper balcony included two hundred seats, but had a maximum capacity of four hundred with the addition of extra chairs. Additionally, the bottom floor contained the first indoor pool built in West Texas, while the second floor housed the basketball floor. The wooden basketball floor was patterned after the original basketball court at Springfield College, where Dr. James Naismith invented the game that is so familiar to us today.

The building was used for gymnastics, various physical education classes, and of course basketball. The physical education program in the 1920s that Marston housed was one of the finest around, led by a long-time Hardin–Simmons staff member Dr. Otho M. Polk, who taught at the university for fifty-one years. Between 1979 and 1980 Marston Gym was remodeled; the major renovation involved the removal of the balcony on the upper level. The uses for the building have changed slightly over time. Marston Gym is now used mainly to accommodate several physical education classes. No matter what the uses, part of Abilene's deep-rooted history will reside within the walls of Marston Gym.

In comparison to the rest of the sprawling and impressive campus of Hardin–Simmons University, the box-like and compact Marston Gym in the center of the photo simply stands watch over the nearby tennis courts and swimming pool on a wet fall day. Notice that the championship Hardin–Simmons Cowboys football team is about to take the field. The houses to the right of the photo are typical examples of the vernacular homes built in north Abilene from the 1920s to the 1960s.

68

Cotton Compress, Abilene, Texas.

AIR VIEW OF TRAFFIC CIRCLE, ABILENE, TEX.

This early 1900s vintage postcard shows the old Western Texas Cotton Compress as it stood on the east side of downtown. Notice the scale in the foreground and the buyer taking the measure of a bale. The majority of the people pictured are African-American, hinting at the important role played by Abilene's black community in the phenomenal success of the West Texas cotton trade in the 1890s to the 1950s. The current cotton warehouse occupying this site went up in the 1920s.

602 North Second Street

by Donald S. Frazier

Cotton used to be king in Abilene. By the turn of the twentieth century, the city could claim at least four major businesses related to the crop, ranging from the venerable H. B. Smith Cotton Gin on the north side of North Fourth Street between Walnut and Pine to the growing Western Texas Cotton Compress emerging on North Second between Plum and Ash street. Farmers produced more than three and a half million bales statewide, with the crop migrating toward the northwest reaches of Texas at a steady pace, eventually spreading out over the rolling plains around Abi-

lene and to the high plains around Lubbock. By 1910 the booming industry had six firms working to turn raw cotton into useful products including the impressive Continental Oil and Cotton Company mill sprawling out on North Fourth between Mesquite and Plum. There were also gins south of the tracks, and eventually even a second seed mill, Abilene Cotton Oil between South Seventh and Eighth along the Abilene and Southern Railroad tracks east of what is now Treadaway Boulevard.

Within three decades of the city's founding downtown had become cotton country. Eventually the volume of business and the bounty of the region created the need for storage facilities for the thousands of bales of cotton and the gallons of oil produced in this commercial faming hub. Warehouses sprang up near railway sidings.

Remarkably, little remains today of this once thriving Abilene industry. The Great Depression, drought, government agriculture policy, and market pressures seriously crimped the cotton industry in Abilene. As a result, firms closed or left town. One of the few reminders of the glory days of white gold are these cotton warehouses from the 1920s that once serviced the Western Texas Cotton Compress operation as they packaged and shipped Abilene's bounty to the rest of the nation.

The cotton warehouse stands in the upper center portion of the 1940s era postcard, and elements from the Western Texas Cotton Compress remain visible. This view toward the northwest also reveals the traffic circle that used to route automobiles into and around downtown from the east. This road feature, now long gone, was located at the present intersection of Business 20 (formerly U.S. Highway 80) and Treadaway Boulevard. The complex to the south of the cotton facility is currently the site of Frontier Texas.

101 Walnut Street

by Derek Peterson

Built in 1906, the Pfeifer Building was originally used as headquarters for H. O. Wooten's wholesale grocery company. This business, established in 1898, gained wide significance and popularity with residents in Abilene and surrounding areas. The building was almost completely destroyed in 1911 by an unexpected and devastating fire, but it was reconstructed the following year. In the renovation, Wooten added an elevator and sprinkler system. By 1948 the company had expanded, creating fourteen branch warehouses throughout the West Texas area.

H.O. Wooten's wholesale grocery company would occupy the structure until the 1950s, when T.S. Langford purchased the building. "T.S. Langford and Sons" was a major employer in Abilene in the 1950s and '60s. The company operated more than 150 sewing machines out of the building, sewing uniforms and work clothing sold all over the country.

Walter Pfeifer Jr. entered into the wholesale business in 1952, gaining great success in manufacturing and selling evaporative coolers in the dry West Texas weather. Pfeifer bought the Wooten Grocery Building in 1967, and the family still owns the building today.

901 North First Street

by Carlos V. Montez

In the mid-nineteenth century, few could have imagined a railroad that would stretch from East Texas all the way to the West Coast. Innovation and ambition were motivating factors that drove upstart capitalists to engage in such a grand endeavor. When most people think about the great railroads of the past, however, few consider that in addition to tracks, passenger stations, and junctions, these companies also needed to build massive freight warehouses.

The Texas & Pacific Railroad Warehouse in Abilene was one of many of its kind built in 1916 alongside the company's route through the southwest. Also known as the T&P Freight Depot, the two-story brick building has an elongated rectangular plan that extends three hundred feet along North First Street. The front entrance faces Pine Street. Large freight loading doors are spaced along the north and south façades. An extensive raised exterior dock runs three hundred feet to the east of the building. The building also has decorative banding below the parapet.

After seventy-five years in its original function, the warehouse was donated by the Union Pacific Railroad Company to the City of Abilene in 1991. The city intended to have the warehouse anchor the Downtown Historic District, creating a corridor for cultural revitalization in the city's center. The warehouse stayed empty for several years, until 1996, when restaurateurs Joe and Sharon Allen leased it from the city to open "The Railhead Grill" at the site. Part of the lease agreement included the city renovating the building at a cost of $1.86 million. Despite these grand plans, the restaurant only survived until 2000, when the Allens decided to shut it down.

The building remained vacant for a couple of years, but in 2003, it became home to The Arrangement, a florist. The retail store is in the front of the building, while the back space is called the "T&P Event Center," available for catered events and receptions. In addition, the event center hosts live music performances and a martini bar a few nights a week. With these changes, the old warehouse truly has become an anchor for the historic downtown area.

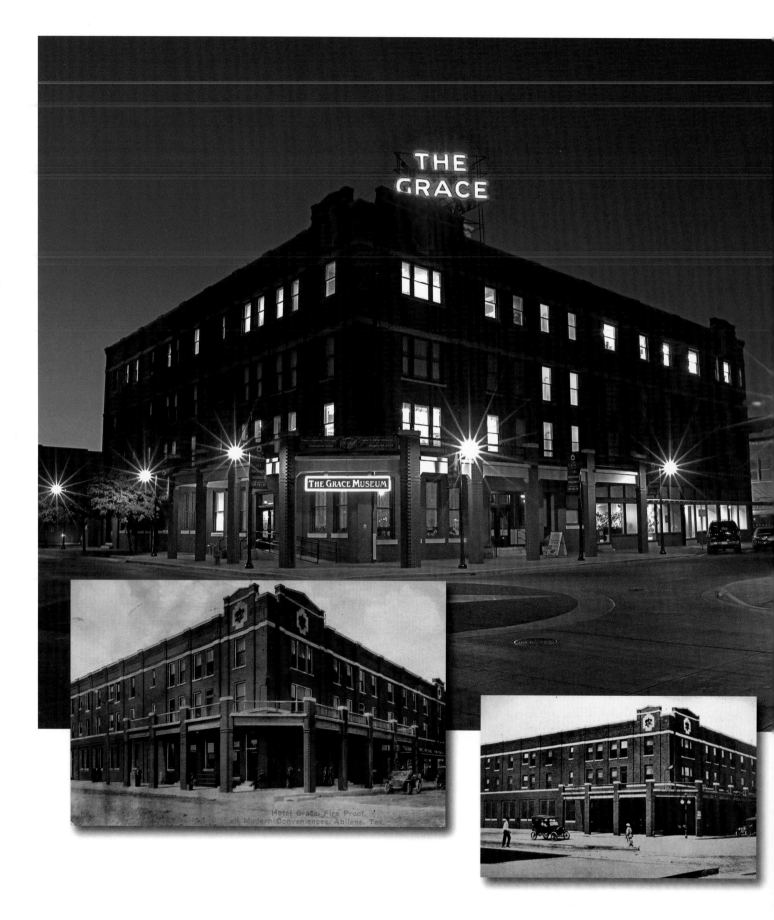

102 Cypress Street

by Emily Young

From the very beginning the Grace has brought many people to Abilene. Starting out in 1909 as Hotel Grace, it quickly became an important asset to West Texas. As the years passed the Grace has changed hands in ownership and purpose, but it has always remained in the hearts of West Texans.

Built by Col. W.L. Beckham, a hotel builder out of Greenville, Texas, the Hotel Grace sat across from the Texas and Pacific Railway Depot and was the only major hotel between Fort Worth and El Paso. Beckham named the hotel after his daughter Grace. Although it started out as a grand hotel it saw its share of hard times.

In the 1940s, after the changing of ownership and the addition of a fourth story, the Grace also got a new name, the Drake. The establishment remained an icon, being host to many parties on the terrace until in the late fifties and early sixties. Then the Drake was no longer such a reputable establishment. It continued to decline until 1973 when it finally closed down after the boiler broke. For twelve years the formerly exquisite hotel deteriorated, but in 1985 the Abilene Preservation League vowed to breathe new life into the condemned building.

The Abilene Preservation League and other Abilenians got together to decide the fate of the historic building. They agreed on a new course, and the city set out to make it a reality. The $4.8 million restoration process brought back the original splendor of the building. It was opened as the Museum of Abilene, housing three separate, but complimentary, museums under one roof. Its importance is infinite for West Texas; it is the only facility of its kind in the twenty-two counties surrounding Abilene.

The Museum of Abilene had a big year in 1998. It paid off the last of the bank loans in February, and its name changed to the Grace Museum, an homage to the building's origins. Its cultural importance is important for West Texans and all who visit Abilene and will continue in that capacity so for many years to come.

75

174 Cypress Street

by Sara Ritson

The oldest commercial building in Abilene, the structure at 174 Cypress Street, began its life as the Windsor Hotel. It was built in 1890 and opened for business in January 1891. Its name was later changed to the Palm Hotel. The grand-looking hotel is three stories high with openings on the second and third floors. The sixteen-foot-high balcony has an impressive wrought-iron railing. The hotel eventually closed because of competition from newer hotels in the downtown area. The Windsor Hotel was then converted into an office building.

During the years after the hotel closed, the structure came under the ownership of many different people and businesses. At one point the building was remodeled so that the exterior of the building was covered by an aluminum false front. In 1997 the structure was restored so that the aluminum front was removed and the original exterior is once again visible. The Cypress Building, sometimes called the Commerce Building, is now the home of the Abilene Chamber of Commerce and the Texas Star Trading Company. The Cypress Building is listed on the National Register of Historic Places.

1174 North First Street

by Ben Newland

In 1913, the Abilene fraternal organization known as the Benevolent and Protective Order of the Elks built their lodge building at 1174 North First Street. The Elks Building, as it became known, contained two large meeting rooms and a grand ballroom. The design of the Elks building is an American-industrial reworking of the Italian Renaissance Style of architecture. In keeping with the style, the architect added large, arched windows wrought with decorative brickwork to accent the area, which also helped bring natural light into the building. Additionally, the flat roof with surrounding clay-tile overhang is a distinct example of Mediterranean influence on the structure's design. In addition to this, the building's boxed shape and overall emphasis on hard right angles, juxtaposed only with the arches of the windows, harkens back to the style of the ancient Roman Villa that so influenced the Italian Renaissance Revival in American Architecture.

The building served as the lodge headquarters for two and a half decades, until dwindling membership numbers forced them to shut it down in 1931. The lodge disbanded, and the building remained largely unused until the advent of World War II. During the war, the Elks Building was converted into a USO recreation center to serve the troops at nearby Camp Barkeley. Since 1945, the City of Abilene has owned the building, using it as both a city hall annex and a police training facility. In 1955 the Elks Lodge regrouped before permanently disbanding in 1964. For a short time the building was known as "Our House" and the Human Relations Center, but in the year 2000, renovation began on the structure and was completed in 2001. Now the building is known as the Elks Art Center and is the headquarters for the Abilene Preservation League.

1101 North First Street

by Anders Jordan Leverton

Due to the westward expansion of railroads in Texas during the nineteenth century, the emergence of the Texas and Pacific Depot in 1881 encouraged the creation of Abilene, which was founded on March 15, 1881. That same day the first train came into town. The T&P Depot was originally a small terminal car, which was replaced by a wooden shanty built by William Slaughter to serve Theodore Heyck's freight business until a better one could be established. Its replacement came in 1910, the building located at 1101 North First Street.

When the current depot was built in, it followed the rules of the time. There were segregated lines for black and white, and they did not disappear until the abolition of the Jim Crow Laws in the 1960s. During World War II, the depot also served as the station where local veterans would ship out and return home, giving the depot, as one could imagine, sentimental value as World War II veterans occasionally return to visit. The building originally had showers and sleeping quarters for workers. In March 1967, the depot's role as a passenger station came to an end, with the last passenger train departing with only 39 travelers headed for Fort Worth.

T. & P. Station, Abilene, Texas.

The Union Pacific Railroad, which took ownership of the T&P Railroad, donated the deed for the depot to the City of Abilene in 1991. Three years later, Abilene renovated the exterior of the depot to resemble its 1910 appearance, and renovated the interior for offices. The former baggage area became a board room and is the only room that still has the original ceiling of the depot. Even though the T&P Depot was built a century ago to promote the City of Abilene, the building still has that function through its current residents—Visitors and Convention Bureau and the Cultural Affairs Council.

1482 North First Street

by Crissi Renaye Reneau

The Old Weather Bureau Building is an important part of Abilene's history. Built by the War Department in 1909 at 1482 North First Street, the bureau soon became attached to the Department of Agriculture. This branch of the federal government monitored weather situations from this building to help advise on crop plantings in the area around Abilene. The Weather Bureau's function was to record the city's temperature, rainfall, wind velocity, and any other important weather detail. To build the structure and buy the land cost $15,176. Five different weather flags could be flown over the building to inform the public about the weather predictions for the day.

The Weather Bureau Building was influenced by several architectural styles, including the Neo-classical, Georgian, and Adam, or Federal, styles. The Adam style was the typical style of this time for weather buildings. The structure is the only federal-style public building that exists in Abilene today, which makes it so significant. The two-story rectangular structure has a full exposed basement, is composed of red brick, has white columnar trim, and boasts a total of three porches. The initial two rooms on the first floor were used as the weatherman's station. The remaining part of the first floor included the family kitchen, dining room, and a pantry. The upstairs included the three bedrooms, a bathroom, and the living room. The basement was used for storage, laundry, and the furnace.

Captain James M. Watson was the first weatherman. A fatal fall or a possible heart attack killed him soon after he arrived, visitors discovering him at the bottom of the basement stairs. On December 19, 1909, William H. Green became the weatherman for the next thirty-four years. He was the longest serving weatherman in Abilene's history.

In 1944 the Weather Bureau moved to the airport; as a result, there were two weather stations for a few years. Then the building was used for storage, and it also housed the Gail Business College. For many years afterward, however, the structure was vacant. In July 1982, the Weather Bureau Building became a historical landmark. The current owners are Cape & Sons, who purchased the building in July of 2002. The commodity merchandising company restored the historic building to its original grandeur.

644 Hickory Street

by Kim Smith

The one-and-a-half-story house at 644 Hickory Street is a wonderful example of the late Victorian-style architecture that was popular at the end of the nineteenth century and the beginning of the twentieth. The wood frame cottage features a hipped roof, gable dormers, and a large front porch. Constructed around 1895 by E.C. Pegues in Old-Town Abilene, the residence was sold to the W.K. Jennings family in 1907. The Jennings family resided there until 1976.

Since the late 1980s, the house has been a café and gift shop. The Victorian Attic gift shop occupies the top floor of the house, while the Hickory Street Café comprises the main floor. The café, known for its chicken salad, zucchini bread, and quiche, is a popular lunch spot in downtown Abilene.

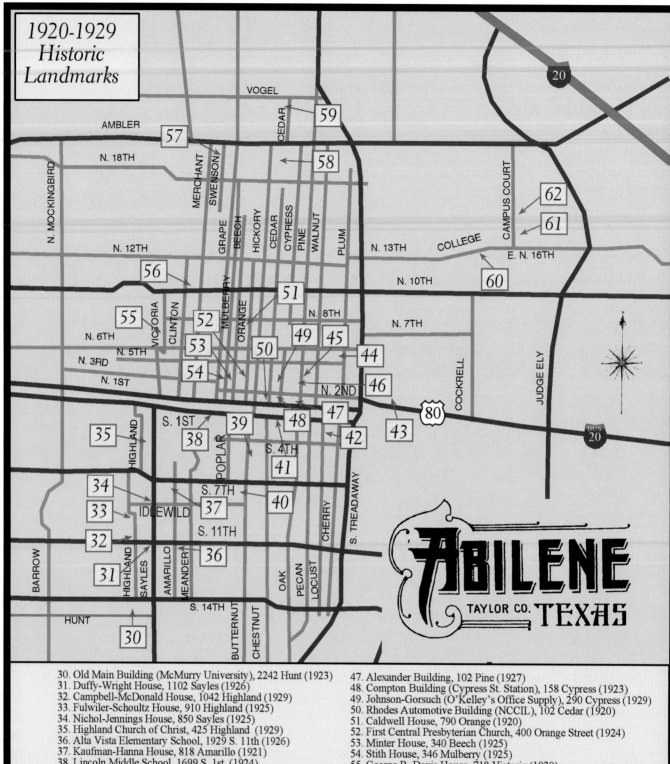

1920-1929 Historic Landmarks

ABILENE TAYLOR CO. TEXAS

30. Old Main Building (McMurry University), 2242 Hunt (1923)
31. Duffy-Wright House, 1102 Sayles (1926)
32. Campbell-McDonald House, 1042 Highland (1929)
33. Fulwiler-Schoultz House, 910 Highland (1925)
34. Nichol-Jennings House, 850 Sayles (1925)
35. Highland Church of Christ, 425 Highland (1929)
36. Alta Vista Elementary School, 1929 S. 11th (1926)
37. Kaufman-Hanna House, 818 Amarillo (1921)
38. Lincoln Middle School, 1699 S. 1st (1924)
39. Old Fire Station #2, 441 Butternut (1926)
40. George W. & Lavina McDaniel House, 774 Butternut (1925)
41. Park Office Building, 901 S. First (1922)
42. Burlington Railroad Depot, 189 Locust (1929)
43. WTU Power and Ice Plant, East Highway 80 (1922)
44. Gulf Distributing Building, 542 Plum (1926)
45. Hilton (Windsor) Hotel, 401 Pine (1927)
46. Minter Building, 244 Pine (1925)

47. Alexander Building, 102 Pine (1927)
48. Compton Building (Cypress St. Station), 158 Cypress (1923)
49. Johnson-Gorsuch (O'Kelley's Office Supply), 290 Cypress (1929)
50. Rhodes Automotive Building (NCCIL), 102 Cedar (1920)
51. Caldwell House, 790 Orange (1920)
52. First Central Presbyterian Church, 400 Orange Street (1924)
53. Minter House, 340 Beech (1925)
54. Stith House, 346 Mulberry (1925)
55. George R. Davis House, 718 Victoria (1920)
56. Abilene Streetcar Barn, 1021 Clinton (1928)
57. Higginbotham House, 2102 Swenson (1920)
58. Hendrick Medical Center, 1900 Pine (1924)
59. Caldwell Hall (HSU), 2418 Cedar St. (1922)
60. Reese-Thornton House, 435 College Drive (1924)
61. Sewell Theatre (ACU), 1625 Campus Court (1929)
62. Zona Luce Hall (ACU), 1755 Campus Court (1929)

· ·

1920–1929

Although it may sound a little clichéd, this amazing American decade was truly a "golden age" for the forty-year-old municipality of Abilene. The city's infrastructure included a reliable water supply, a large power plant, a streetcar line, a fabulous park and fair ground, and other amenities that indicated that the city was up to date and moving toward a great destiny. Business was booming, including the cotton industry, ranch and real estate enterprises, and the beginnings of petroleum and railroad-based fortunes. A third college had opened as well. The churches and homes that remain from this era radiate prosperity, just like the electric lights that graced their ceilings.

87

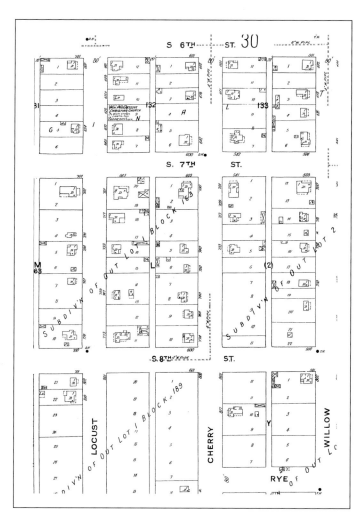

A 1925 south side neighborhood in Abilene, including the "Non-Progressive Christian Church"

The Old Main building at McMurry University started out known as the Administration Building. This photo from the 1980s shows the venerable building presiding over a beautiful spring day from its position on the south side of the quadrangle. The authors of this book have offices on the second floor on the left, or northeastern, corner of the building with a sweeping view of the campus.

This postcard dates to the early days of McMurry College. Two of the buildings shown, marked Main Building and Girls' Dormitory, remain. While the first of these two is an icon of the institution and is pictured on the official school seal, the other has been incorporated into the much larger President's Dorm that graces the campus today. Administrators ordered the windows seen on the end of Old Main to be bricked over in the 1980s to reduce the utility costs of heating and cooling the building.

2242 Hunt Street

by KC Walters

Plans for the third church-affiliated college in Abilene began in the early 1920s. As the first president, J.W. Hunt oversaw construction on the new administration building, which began in April 1922. Designed by prominent local architect, David Castle, the building rested on a portion of the forty-two acres of land donated by Judge K.K. Legett, J.M. Cunningham, and Henry Sayles. David Castle successfully completed the building by August of 1923, a month before classes officially began, September 19, 1923.

When McMurry opened its doors in 1923, the three-story Administration Building housed everything but the dormitories. The light brick classical revival structure stands tall and demands attention from the visitors of the campus. Inside, the floor and interior woodwork, as well as the doors and staircase were made of golden maple. The top floor housed the science laboratories and the fine arts department, which included studios and several practice rooms. The library and several classrooms filled the second floor, as balcony access for the auditorium. The first floor had still more classrooms, all the administrative offices, and the auditorium. As the college grew, the lack of space in the building forced classrooms and departments to move out. The structure encountered a lot of wear and tear and the maintenance crew completed minor repairs and renovations over the years.

The administration planned a massive renovation in 1983 with more than one million dollars raised. In order to install central heating and air, the plans included lowered ceilings. The plans also included filling in the windows on the sides and back of the structure. The whole building needed patching and painting. Many of the classrooms turned into offices.

"Old Main," as the building became known over the years, has served McMurry well for more than eighty years and will continue to do so for years to come. Today, the building has some classrooms, and it houses several academic and student services departments, as well as faculty and staff offices.

89

1102 Sayles Boulevard

by Ben Hoyng

The Duffy-Wright House is a unique home that stands out even among the variety of luxurious and historical homes on Sayles Boulevard. This house, located at 1102 Sayles, features interesting architecture. Built in 1926 the front of the home boasts white pillars that hold up the building's roof among the structure's deep red bricks and white lattice windows. It also features nearly 3,200 square feet of living space, plus a carport, open porch, and detached garage with apartment—all original to the house.

One of the most noticeable aspects of the Duffy-Wright House is the peculiar front yard. It has a dogleg ramp on both sides, taking up most of the yard with the ramp continuing to the driveway along edge of the home. This unique home is truly a landmark among landmarks on Sayles Boulevard.

1042 Highland Avenue

by Ben Hoyng

The Campbell-McDonald House at 1042 Highland is a distinctive-looking home built in 1929. The house's architecture is based on the Spanish Colonial style, which was very popular in the early twentieth century. The tan, one-story home features earth-orange terra cotta shingles on the roof as well as in the pathways to the front door and the backyard. The 3,200-square-foot house also has a detached garage with apartment, all original construction in 1929. There are also many small, distinctive details that make the house stand out, such as the sculpted face installed over the entrance, or the molding that looks like small columns running up the walls.

The Campbell-McDonald House is also a historical landmark in Abilene for another reason. It was the first house to be built fully wired for electricity. West Texas Utilities used this house as a demonstration for the rest of Abilene of how an electric home works. The house is prestigious for helping the Abilene community while contributing to the architecture that shows Abilene's changes in the early twentieth century.

910 Highland Avenue

by Terann Ragland

There is a beautiful illustration of the profound history of Abilene hidden in the Alta Vista neighborhood at 910 Highland. This remarkable home sits on a strip of land just over 1.2 acres. William J. Fulwiler, owner of the Fulwiler Electric Company, built the home in 1925. A civic leader and businessman, Fulwiler wanted to have a grand home on a spacious lot. He succeeded. The structure features a main living area of more than 4,600 square feet. Also original to the grounds are a detached storage unit and garage, as well as a spacious open porch. The wonderfully ornate décor on the front of the home adds to the value, as well as the beautiful, soaring columns towering over the property. The home is now owned by V.H. Schoultz, M.D.

850 Sayles Boulevard

by Crissi Renaye Reneau

The Nichol-Jennings House at 850 Sayles Boulevard is reminiscent of a fairy tale. The house, on the southwest corner of Idlewild Street and Sayles Boulevard, stands out even among the other important homes in the region. It has a tower, which makes it one of a kind.

W.J. Nichol built this house in 1926 for his family. A local architect in the Abilene area, Nichol built his home in the Spanish Revival style popular in the region in the 1920s. He did, however, add the special feature of a tower through which the front door enters the house. The home boasts just over 1,600 square feet of living space and a detached garage, original to the house in 1925. The cream-colored brick house also features a roof made of clay tile. This truly unique house adds a whimsical delight to the historic Sayles Boulevard.

425 Highland Avenue

by Ben Hoyng

The Highland Church of Christ's history goes back to the turn of the twentieth century. In 1903 twenty-seven adults met at the old Taylor County Courthouse to organize a congregation. The group began meeting in a building on South Sixth and Chestnut Street and was known as the "Local Congregation."

Eventually the group was invited to worship in the administration building of the Abilene Christian College on North First Street. The group became known as the "College Congregation," but in 1928, college officials decided to move the campus to the northeast side of the city. The College Congregation decided to move with the college, but some fifty members wanted to continue to worship on the south side of town, within walking distance of their homes. Abilene Christian College deeded some land on North First to these members, who sold the property and purchased a lot at 449 Highland Avenue. In 1928, the church paid Abilene Construction Company $2,450 to construct a building. The new building was ready for worship in 1929.

Over the decades since that first worship service in the new building, the Highland Church of Christ congregation has continued to grow and has continued to add onto the building. It has now become an important landmark in a historic section of the city.

1929 South Eleventh Street

by Tiffany Lynn Grove

Tears ran down the faces of the students and teachers of Alta Vista Elementary School at the end of the 2002-2003 school year. Due to a large drop in student enrollments in the city's public schools, the Abilene Independent School District trustees decided on January 30, 2003, that the closing of several schools, including Alta Vista on 1929 South Eleventh Street, was necessary.

Construction for the one-story traditional, red-bricked elementary was completed in 1926. Alta Vista consists of four buildings. The main structure, which faces South Eleventh Street, has a sloped roof and a red-bricked chimney, while the others have flat roofs. All have long orange-outlined windows to match the orange walkways, which connect the edifices together. A huge light blue steel gymnasium and a playground stand behind these buildings.

When Alta Vista was an elementary, it housed classrooms for pre-kindergarten to sixth grades. Its location attracted economically diverse students because houses that ranged from $20,000 to $200,000 surrounded the campus. Of its approximately four hundred students, seventy percent were on the free or reduced lunch program.

By the start of the 21st Century, however, demographic changes altered the fate of Alta Vista. In a three-year period at the start of the new century, Abilene lost around 1,500 students. Consequently, AISD lost $4 million in state aid. Therefore, the school district trustees chose to close various schools, including Alta Vista.

But the doors would not remain closed for long. The school board decided to continue using the building for an educational function. Today, it is the district's Adult Learning Center.

818 Amarillo Street
by Crissi Renaye Reneau

In 1921, Mr. and Mrs. S.E. Kaufman built the house at 818 Amarillo Street. Mr. Kaufman came to work as the secretary of Percy Jones, a railroad executive and city father in Abilene.

The house is built in the Arts and Craftsman style, which became popular during the 1920s, and was inspired by the Green Brothers in California. The Arts and Craftsman style offered pre-cut lumber packages and instructions of assembly for a local contractor. The Craftsman style can also overlap with the Bungalow, Mission, or a Prairie style home.

On occasions, the Kaufmans would have a special visit by a local little girl by the name of Judy Jones, who lived at 602 Amarillo Street. Judy was the daughter of Percy Jones. Judy liked to visit the Kaufmans, and on several occasions, she recalled that she would slide down the Kaufmans' hallway in her socks. Now known as Judy Jones Matthews, she has been an important contributor to the Abilene community. Judy Jones Matthews was chosen as the Abilenean of the Millennium in 2000 by the Abilene Reporter-News for her efforts to restore historic buildings in the city.

The lovely historic home at 818 Amarillo Street is the current residence of Dr. Carl Trusler and Dr. Jaynne Middleton. They are the seventh owners of this beautiful home. Jaynne loved high ceilings, the spacious rooms, and the double front porch of the house. But the large kitchen was their favorite room because it "accommodates two serious cooks with good functionality." In 2004 the current owners did an extensive restoration on their home, which included the kitchen, den, hall, staircase, bathrooms, and the first floor bedroom. They used quarter-sawn white oak and authentic Craftsman period colors to match to the time period of the 1920s style, color, and quality. This beautiful home has been part of the Abilene Preservation League's Fall Home Tour, and it is definitely worth a visit.

High School, Abilene, Texas.

Abilene Senior High School
Abilene, Texas

This impressive structure depicted in this postcard went up sometime shortly after 1910 on the northwest corner of Peach and South Third. First serving as Abilene High School, it transitioned to a junior high when a newer building went up in 1924 just a block away, facing South First. This red brick landmark remained an important part of the educational landscape for decades before giving way to the voracious space demands of its growing neighbor.

1699 South First Street

by Joseph Trey Cox, III

"Enter To Learn, Go Forth To Serve." This motto is written on a brass plaque, which adorns the entry way of Lincoln Middle School. Originally Abilene High School, the old brick building on South First Street stands majestically as time passes her by. In the fall of 1954, the building became Lincoln Junior High, when Abilene High School moved to its present building. The building remained in continuous use as a junior high/middle school from that time until 2007, when the AISD built a new middle school on the southeast side of the city.

Since 1889 the site, which is now Lincoln Middle School, has been used for educational purposes. A public school sat on the corner of South First and Peach in 1896, being designated Abilene High School by 1902. Six years later, the structure wore the name Central Ward School; old pictures show wood-framed buildings clustered at this location. By 1915 a newly raised red brick structure at the northwest corner of Peach and South Third became the home of Abilene High School. In less than a decade administrators demoted this once adequate structure to a junior high after the 1924 construction of the current building fronting South First.

Architect David S. Castle designed the structure to be built with steel support beams, lending a sense of permanence to the school. Many additions and renovations have been completed since the opening. The band hall, among other additions, was built within the first five years of the school's existence. In 1970s the school district built a girls' gym on the south side of the building. Eventually the complex dominated the entire block, erasing all but faint traces of the earlier learning facilities that once stood there. With all the additions throughout the years the main building itself has not been substantially changed. Some interior work has been completed in order to update the structure with the changing times.

High School, Abilene, Texas

1A3242

When the school district decided to build a new middle school in 2004, many members of the community did not want to see Lincoln Middle School destroyed. Some suggested making it part of the Grace Museum or using it to display Abilene school history. In early 2008, the school board voted to add a major bond issue to the public with the idea of renovating Lincoln into the district's career technology campus. Whatever the outcome, it is clear that Lincoln will remain part of this community for many years to come.

441 Butternut Street

by Joseph Trey Cox, III

Before Abilene had any underpasses connecting the north and south sides of the city, the railroad tracks that were the lifeblood of the community presented a major hazard for residents living south of them. Abilene's original fire station was on the north side. If a train sat on the tracks and a fire broke out to the south, there was no way to get the equipment to the blaze in time to quench the flames.

In the early 1920s Abilene's boom made it hard on the city's government to provide adequate fire protection for the citizens. Mayor Charles E. Coombes led the way in 1926, authorizing the construction Abilene's second fire station. He also converted the Fire Department from an all-volunteer crew to a full-time, professional organization. The cost of construction topped $10,550, but with these changes, Abilene citizens had a much greater sense of safety in their sprawling city.

After several decades, the city built several other stations to serve the growing population, and the Old Fire Station #2 was sold and then later abandoned. The structure has seen many different businesses come and go throughout its history. Attorneys Jeff Lewis and Gary Connally bought it in 1990, with intentions to renovate it as the office of their law firm. They were disappointed that the original fire pole had been lost from the structure, so they located a similar pole from a fire station in Colorado. They had it shipped in and installed between the floors of the building. They have seen to it, however, that the hole is covered in a transparent plastic to avoid any potential injuries at the site. In the renovation, the attorneys also found the original gas pump and underground tank. With an eye toward the environment, they removed the tank, but the pump still remains. Now listed on the National Register of Historic Places, this important Abilene landmark should be around for decades to come.

#40 George W. and Lavina McDaniel House (1925)

· ·

774 Butternut Street

by Robert F. Pace

In 1891 the 700 block of Butternut was well south of the majority of homes and businesses in Abilene. In that year, however, George W. McDaniel, Sr., built a beautiful Victorian home at 774 Butternut.

A few decades later, his son George Jr., married and took ownership of the home. A newspaperman, George Jr. had risen quickly into the management of the *Abilene Reporter-News*. He and his wife, Lavina, decided to tear down the old family home in 1925 and replace it with this stately Prairie-style house at the same location. In constructing their new home, however, the McDaniels reused most of the lumber, doors, and windows from the original Victorian house.

This noble house features more than four thousand square feet of living space and a large open front porch. In 1977 the Junior League of Abilene purchased the house for its headquarters. The Junior League of Abilene completed extensive interior renovations, saving this structure as an important Abilene landmark.

This photo shows the Park Office Building before new owners expanded it to the west, or right, in this picture.

901 South First Street

by Catherine Ann Watjen and Gail Adlesperger

By the 1920s, Abilene had grown into a considerable West Texas community. During this "Golden Era," J.M. and D.E. Radford built this landmark in 1922. The Radford family financed the construction of many Abilene buildings during the 1920s. The Park Building, located at 901 South First, is the only building of its age remaining intact along the line of buildings facing the tracks. This $100,000 structure was designed by the David Castle Architectural Firm, perhaps the most important of Abilene's early designers. The Park Office Building remained a key office building for numerous years.

The design and structure of the building has Neoclassical detailing. The classical-styled exterior was constructed in face brick with white limestone trim. The building has very similar features in its structure as was going on in Chicago between 1890 and 1930. The inspiration for this style was churches and palaces of the Renaissance in Italy.

The first tenant of the structure was Abilene Building and Loan. In its early years after construction, the Park Office Building was also used as a women's business college. It the late 30s and early '40s, the Abilene Chamber of Commerce moved into the site, then after World War II a clothing manufacturer took over the building. Since then, the building has been used by businesses such as the United States Treasury, the Texas Employment Service, and Abilene Beauty School. The building was unoccupied until 1965 when Zachry Printing and Advertising took residence. In the late 1960s and early 1970s, E-Z Serve Inc. took on the task of refurbishing the interior of the building. It changed much of the interior space into offices, while preserving the exterior. Skinny's Convenience Food Stores also had its general office for food brokers here in the 1980s.

In 1996, Lauren Construction purchased the building when they moved their headquarters from Atlanta, Georgia, to Abilene. To accommodate their needs, the company has made several improvements, such as the installation of an elevator, and an expansion of the building to the west in 2007, doubling the office space available. With its ornate doors and the beautiful canopy hanging over the entrance, the Park Office Building is still an impressive landmark in Abilene.

189 Locust Street

by Derek Peterson

Col. Morgan Jones, sometimes called the "Father of Texas Railroads," was responsible for the train depot located at 189 Locust. Jones constructed numerous short railroad lines that connected many growing cities in Texas, up through Colorado and into Denver. By the time he had died in 1926, Texas contained about fifty railroad properties with more than sixteen thousand miles of track. At that time, these figures accounted for one-fortieth of all the worlds' railroad lines.

One of Jones's projects after the creation of Abilene was to build the Abilene and Northern Railway Company, which contained thirty-eight miles of track between Abilene and Stamford, Texas, to the north. The first building at 189 Locust was known as the Abilene and Northern Depot. In 1907, however, the Burlington Railroad Company purchased the Abilene and Northern, linking tracks all the way north to Illinois. In 1929, the Burlington Company constructed the current depot, replacing the original wooden structure that had stood at the site. The new depot was built in the Spanish Colonial Revival and remains a testament to the once-vital railroads that connected Abilene to the world.

#43 WEST TEXAS UTILITIES POWER & ICE PLANT (1922)

East Highway 80 & 100 Block North Second

by Derek Peterson

The first use of electric lights in Abilene, Texas, occurred around 1891. This innovation of electricity in homes and businesses created a greater demand for this new resource. Between 1912 and 1922, a multitude of remote utility companies in the western part of Texas were contributing to the local power system. American Public Service Company completed construction of the power plant at East Highway 80 on October 25, 1922, after the loss of Abilene's first power plant in a devastating fire. The original plant had been located in the vicinity of Plum Street between North Third and North Fourth.

The building is a commercialized industrial structure that reflects the sign of the times with its brick piers and the banding formations, which create large rectangular patterns throughout this structure. The most recognized landmark structure at the facility is the tall stack that towers over the landscape and can be seen from various areas of the region.

Abilene Electric and Power became the West Texas Utilities Power and Ice plant in 1923. The power plant produced ice for iceboxes, the major means for keeping food fresh in residences of the day. The ice plant became obsolete by 1942 because of the increased availability of modern electric refrigeration units for the home. This plant remained operational through 1963, when it was finally retired.

542 Plum Street

by Michael Jerry Akin

In 1926 the sounds of pumps running, meters turning, men shouting to open this valve or that one would have provided the backdrop for the work conditions at the Gulf Distribution Building. Tracks still line the front of the building where rail cars full of petroleum products would have pulled up and unloaded into storage tanks. Workers loaded trucks with petroleum products to be delivered to the Gulf service stations in Abilene and surrounding communities. This process seemed routine and habitual, but the Gulf Distribution Building provided a steady, honest income for Abilenians for years.

Owner J.Y. Biggerstaff constructed the building, located at 542 Plum Street, in 1926. At first, Biggerstaff's distribution center served only two stations in Abilene—one at 1140 North Fifth Street, and the other at the southeast corner of South First Street and Butternut, known as "Station Number Two."

From only two stations in 1926, Biggerstaff's business increased dramatically in just five years. By 1931 the Gulf Distribution Building supplied nine stations. With each additional Gulf station, Biggerstaff's company took on more employees.

From the 1930s through the 1960s, the distribution building had several managers, including W.P. Wright, Al G. Phillips, and Grady Hughes. By the 1970s, however, the Gulf Corporation fell on hard times. Then in 1984, the Gulf board voted to sell the company to Chevron for $13.2 Billion. It was the largest corporate merger to date. With this buy-out the building on Plum Street went vacant. In 2001, Jeff Luther Construction renovated the structure and made the building its headquarters.

401 Pine Street

by Leah Herod

Did you know that Abilene once had the first hotel to bear the famous name Hilton? The elegant nine-story structure on 401 Pine Street began life as the first Hilton Hotel, but it is now known as the Windsor. Whatever the building is called, it has had a lasting impression, serving as a visible connection to Abilene's past.

In the early 1890s Abilene's economy depended primarily on cotton and cattle, until 1918 when oil discoveries in neighboring counties brought wildcatters and traders to Abilene. A group of Abilenians recognized the need for a large new hotel that could support the increasing business activity. In 1926 thirteen prominent businessmen took the first step toward making this dream a reality by signing a petition pledging five to ten thousand dollars each in an effort to spark interest within the community. The plan worked—pledges from local citizen investors rose to more than $350,000.

David S. Castle, a prominent Abilene architect, was selected to build the hotel. He created a ten-floor, light-tan brick building with a flat roof. It features twenty-seven bay windows that are evenly spaced at the bottom. The outside structure includes classical details in cream-colored terra-cotta. The building is basic in design; its only decoration is a band around the second and ninth floors with a simple cornice.

Conrad Hilton, a young man who operated a small hotel in Cisco, Texas, was selected to run Abilene's new hotel. Trying to establish his name, Hilton used it in Abilene, and the Hilton Hotel opened on September 21, 1927. The Hilton Hotel set a "new standard for luxury." As Abilene's tallest building of its day, it demanded attention and was noticeably visible to railroad passengers arriving at the depot only four blocks away.

The hotel served as a well-known social location as Abilene continued to grow. The Hilton social scene flourished as bands played music in the famous dining room and hotel restaurant. The most stunning space was the mezzanine floor where the grand ballroom was located. A beautiful hardwood floor, three crystal chandeliers, and nine huge arched windows graced the grand ballroom. Three balconies in the ballroom, as well as the second floor, overlook the marbled lobby.

In 1945 Abilene stockholders took control of the hotel, and changed the name to Windsor after the old hotel on North Second and Cypress. Keeping the Windsor name alive, most Abilenians know the hotel by this name. Two years later, the Windsor was sold to the Harrison Interests.

A developer purchased the Windsor in the 1980s with plans of transforming the hotel into executive suites. Without proper funding, this project ended incomplete, and the Windsor sat vacant for almost a decade. In 1992 Bill

(continued)

Wenson purchased the property with the idea of creating apartments for low-income senior citizens. Tony Eeds, an expert on historic restoration, was selected to refurbish the Windsor. The building underwent gutting and complete restoration in 1993.

On January 1, 1994, it opened as housing for senior citizens, and Abilene demonstrated once again its love for the Windsor. Abilene has saved a historic landmark that has been so much a part of its history. Created and kept alive by Abilenians, the Windsor serves a "perfect blend of Yesterday's Memories and Tomorrow's Dreams."

Hotel Hilton, Abilene, Texas

SKY LINE OF ABILENE, TEXAS

3A-H1161

121

THE HILTON HOTEL, ABILENE, TEXAS.   118334

244 Pine Street

by Kensey Robert Allen

The Minter Building has long stood in the middle of downtown Abilene and is now part of the Abilene Commercial Historic District. In 1925 architect David S. Castle worked with Balfanz Construction Company to build this commercial structure for G.F. Brittain. It is a two-story masonry retail store with Gothic detailing, a pointed-arch motif, and a five-part configuration on the ground floor. It is one of David S. Castle and Company's finest commercial designs in Abilene. It contains outer and central bays with display windows while other bays provide access to the interior. The building housed Minter Dry Goods Store, one of Abilene's best-known retail establishments, from 1926 to 1940.

Today the building maintains its original charm. The second floor still retains its three-bay configuration with three windows per bay. The bottom floor has been altered throughout the years as businesses have come and gone. The entryway into the building is covered with glass with displays reminiscent of old department store fronts.

The building is currently owned by Cindy McCathren, who opened an arts and crafts cooperative named Under One Roof. Walking in the doors, one is bombarded with sights of crafts, jewelry, antiques, and other gift ideas on display throughout the store. McCathren also operates "The Loft," a sandwich shop and catering business located on the second floor of the building. The down-home atmosphere takes the visitor back to the building's origin. Walking through the old Minter Building, one cannot help but picture just what it must have been like during the building's prime.

The Alexander Building under construction, looking west down North First Street. The Grace Hotel is barely visible in the background.

102 Pine Street

by Carlos V. Montez

What does the word "Skyscraper" bring to mind—tall buildings in New York City? Even before there was an Empire State Building, Abilene had the new Alexander Building, its first skyscraper, in 1927.

On March 2, 1924, Dr. J. M. Alexander announced plans for a seven-story office building to be the tallest in town—a full three stories higher than the nearby Citizens National Bank Building. Designed by David Castle's architectural firm, the building promised to "eclipse any office building in West Texas exclusive of Wichita Falls." The builder was Walsh and Burney of San Antonio. Dr. Alexander, who had begun practicing medicine in Abilene as early as 1901, and who founded the Alexander Sanitarium, maintained an office in his namesake building until his death.

The architectural detail of the building displays a prominent cornice, large first- floor bays, and stone facing. Its style is from several types, including Chateauesque or Beaux Arts, and Neoclassical architecture. Neoclassical became a dominant style for domestic buildings nationwide between 1900 and the 1940s. It was directly inspired by the Beaux-Arts style and the Columbian Exposition: classical symmetry, full-height porch with columns and temple front; classical ornament. Fundamentally, this pattern was a return to the Greek Revival style.

Despite these nods to other styles, the Alexander Building has many unique characteristics and one-of-kind qualities. Today, the seven-story brick-veneered office building houses several local businesses and area law firms. The Alexander Building is an important landmark that represents an architectural phase that swept the United States from 1900 to the 1940s and found its way to West Texas.

PINE STREET, ABILENE, TEXAS, LOOKING NORTH

This late 1920s postcard provides a glimpse northward up Pine Street. The new Alexander Building stands tall to the left, while the first ever Hilton Hotel stands in the distance to the right of the roadway. Notice that the tracks are even with the street, and the trolley tracks coursing down the middle of Pine. What is now Everman Park is to the lower left, and the bright red T&P Freight Warehouse stands in the lower right. Abilene, from all appearances, was a prosperous town at the time of this image.

158 Cypress Street

by Sara Ritson

The Compton Building at 158 Cypress Street was constructed in 1923. The first tenants for the building were a drugstore and cleaners on the first floor with offices for doctors and dentists on the second floor. The Compton Building also hosted a pool hall. The building became vacant in the mid 1930s until the 1950s when a lighting fixture store opened. In 1970, the property once again became vacant. During the times when the building was not in use, it was used as a storage site for the surrounding buildings.

In 1992 work to restore the building began, taking about a year to complete. In 1993 the Compton Building was ready to open its doors again, this time as a restaurant, the Cypress Street Station. The restoration brought the building back to its original splendor. With the exception of the arches running through the middle of the restaurant for support, everything has been restored so the building is the same as when the drugstore was in business. Some of the repairs consisted of correcting the damage done to the building by time and weather during the years it was empty. The restaurant has entertained many well-known faces, including presidents, congressmen, and governors. The Compton Building, listed on the National Register of Historic Places, is an important part of Abilene's historic downtown district.

290 Cypress Street

by Catherine Ann Watjen

By simply walking into the Johnson and Gorsuch Building at 290 Cypress, one can feel its past all around. Its history runs through the original maplewood floors all the way to the fans that cooled the space in decades past. In 1929 Balfanz Construction built this structure at a cost of $90,000, and from that time to now, this building has celebrated several businesses that are well known and used by the citizens of Abilene.

Two Abilene businesses held claim to the space on 290 Cypress Street from 1929 to 1959. G.W. Waldrop and Co., or Waldrop's Furniture as it is more commonly known, was the landmark's first owner. In 1934, however, Waldrop's moved a few blocks over, and Montgomery Ward moved in. The department store held the space and served Abilene for twenty-five years. After Montgomery Ward left in 1959, the Johnson and Gorsuch Building remained empty until 1967, when O'Kelley's Office Supply moved in.

O'Kelley's Office Supply has served Abilene ever since. Their loving ownership of the building has helped to keep it well preserved and in excellent condition. This building on Cypress Street maintains its historical integrity and remains one of Abilene's historical treasures.

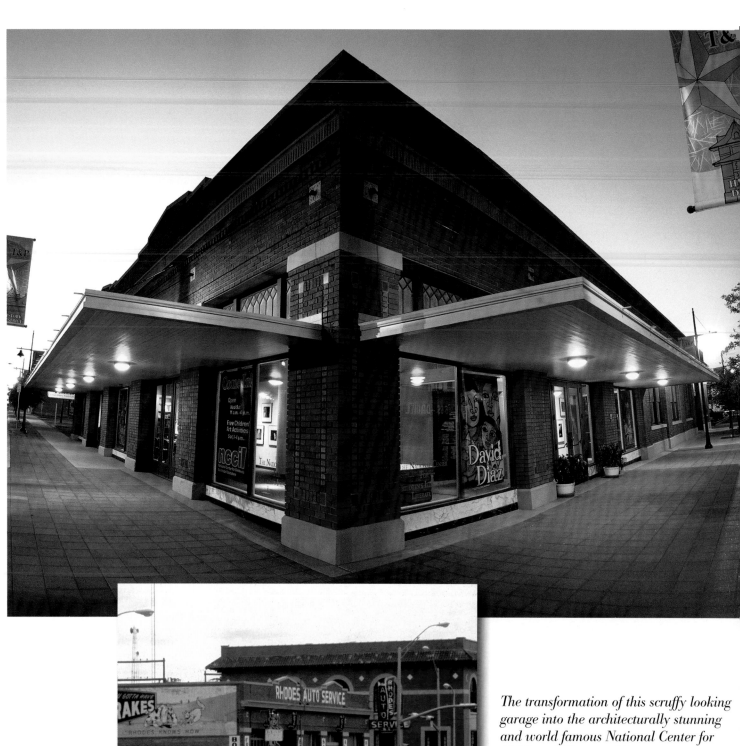

The transformation of this scruffy looking garage into the architecturally stunning and world famous National Center for Childrens' Illustrated Literature (NCCIL) is a true historic preservation success story coupled with the creation of a great cultural landmark.

102 Cedar Street

by Emily Young

What is the significance of an old garage? In 1920 the building at 102 Cedar represented a new era—the age of the automobile. In a decade when motor transportation was becoming more easily available to the average family, garages took the place in society previously held by stables and blacksmiths.

But what can be done with an abandoned garage that is nearly eighty years old? The citizens of Abilene answered this question by giving the old garage on Cedar a new purpose. The building is now home to the National Center for Children's Illustrated Literature (NCCIL).

The renovation of the garage into the NCCIL was a collaborative effort of the Junior League of Abilene, the Museums of Abilene, and a community, state, and nationally based steering committee. The center houses a gallery to hold exhibits for illustrators and recognition of their work. It also provides education and awareness for children's literacy.

In 1993 Abilene Mayor Gary McCaleb was reading story, "Santa Calls," to a local elementary school. As he was reading he took notice of the beautiful illustrations. After leaving he decided to call the illustrator, William Joyce. When the two met later that year at a conference they immediately formed an alliance. It wasn't long until the two had come up with the idea for the NCCIL.

The Junior League took charge of the project and committed to raise the two million dollars it would take to renovate the Rhodes Garage. In 2000 their efforts paid off, and the NCCIL opened its doors to the public. Now the building will be useful for generations to come.

790 Orange Street

by KC Walters

The Caldwell House at 790 Orange Street, built in 1920, is easily the grandest house still standing in the Parramore District. The third house built in the neighborhood, it was the first to be recognized in Abilene's Historic Landmark. It was granted Historic Overlay Zoning in March of 1985.

E.V. and Susan Sellers built their second home in 1920 for $50,000. Colonel J.H. Parramore founded the Parramore district when he bought the area in 1882. Upon his death in 1917 he divided up the land into six blocks giving one to each of his children. Ray Boatright, Abilene's premier architect of the time, began building the house in 1919 for Susan Sellers and finished in 1920. The Sellers lived in the house less than a year and sold it to W.C. Goodwin in 1921 for $25,000. Goodwin in turn sold the house for the same price a year later in 1922 to C.M. Caldwell. The Caldwells lived in the house for forty years.

The Caldwell house is a Prairie style home, easily the biggest of that style in the Parramore District neighborhood. The house is seven thousand square feet, including the carriage house/apartment behind the main house. The house features large porches on the first and second floors. The bottom floor encompasses a dining room, living room, solarium, large hall, breakfast room, kitchen, utility room, den, master bedroom and bath. A climb up the stairs or a ride up the elevator brings into view the second floor, which has five bedrooms, two bathrooms, and a large hall or den. The Caldwells converted the carriage house in the back to an apartment to rent out during the days of the depression. The interior of the house is very much unaltered and all of the interior appointments are intact.

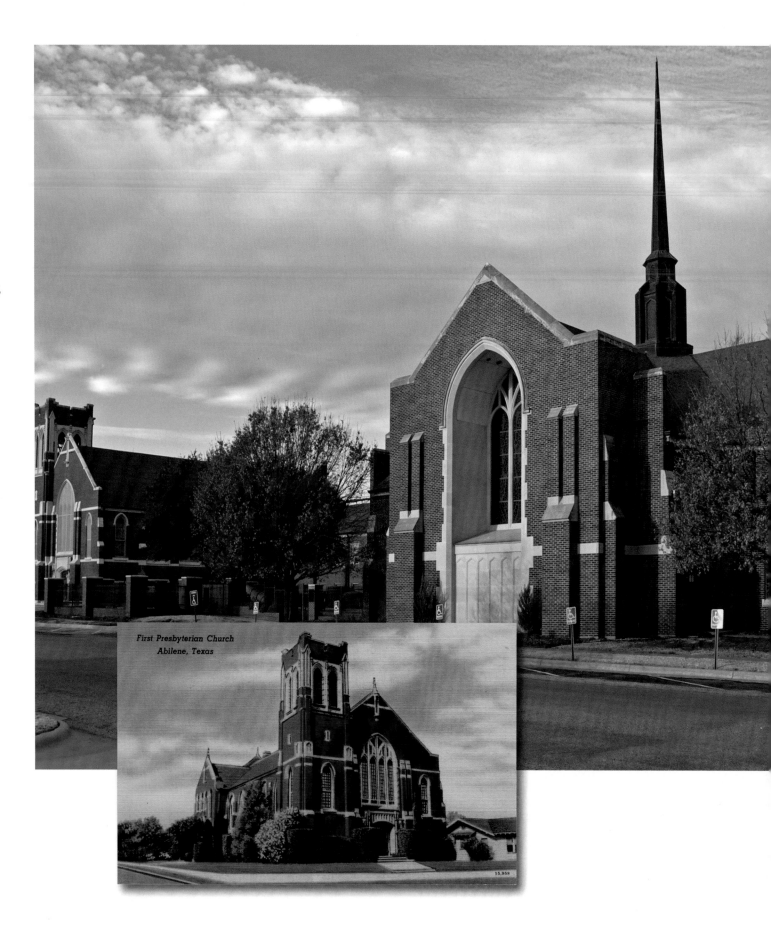

First Presbyterian Church
Abilene, Texas

400 Orange Street

by Ben Newland

On February 27, 1881, in what was to become Everman Park, the congregation that would eventually build the First Central Presbyterian Church held their first big-tent church service, one of the first worship services in town. Meeting sites came and went, until, thirty-seven years later, Abilene's Central and First Presbyterian Churches began to hold services jointly under the leadership of Dr. T.S. Knox.

In 1920, the two congregations voted to part ways but still remain closely tied. Nevertheless, Dr. Knox supervised the construction of a new church building in 1924 and preached the first sermon held within its walls. This structure would become the south end of the current First Central Presbyterian Church's campus, encompassing the classrooms and fellowship hall.

In 1950, prompted by a doubling in Abilene's population, the church began construction of the present Education Building, which was completed in 1954. The First and Central Presbyterian Churches reunited in 1970 under the leadership of Dr. Roy Zuefeldt, and in 1976, the church initiated the building program to construct the current sanctuary and renovate the old sanctuary for a fellowship hall. From this point until 2000, the church continued to add new structures as they felt led, and, hence, the structure we see today.

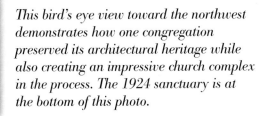

This bird's eye view toward the northwest demonstrates how one congregation preserved its architectural heritage while also creating an impressive church complex in the process. The 1924 sanctuary is at the bottom of this photo.

340 Beech Street

by Sara Ritson

William A. Minter, Jr., was born in Mississippi in 1871. When he was eight years old, his father moved the family to Buffalo Gap, Texas. With the founding of Abilene two years later in 1881, the Minters made their home in the new city. In 1900, Minter opened Minter Dry Goods Company, which later changed its name to Minter's Department Store. As well as owning a successful store and making many other contributions to Abilene, Minter helped organize the First Presbyterian Church and helped establish a locally owned gas company. He died in 1935.

During the height of Abilene's 1920s "Golden Age," Minter constructed this house on Beech Street as his family home. The two-story, brick Tudor Revival style house was designed by an Abilene architectural firm, Nichols and Campbell. Today, this impressive structure is listed on the National Register of Historic Places.

Fittingly, the building is now owned by the Tittle-Luther Partnership Offices, one of Abilene's most prolific architectural firms. As the only surviving residential building owned by Minter, the house is an important reminder of Abilene's early history.

346 Mulberry Street

by Mandy Elson

139

The Stith House, located at 346 Mulberry in Abilene, Texas, is famous for its wood-shingled roof that gives the house a thatched-like appearance. This house has enriched Abilene with its architectural design and through the works of the original owner, Will Stith.

Will Stith was a successful local businessman involved in many commercial ventures. Born in Jackson County, Missouri, in April 24, 1856, he later moved to Galveston, Texas. He engaged in clerking a wholesale and retail grocery for eight years and attended school at night acquiring a position as a bookkeeper with the firm of Clark & Courts. In 1887, he married Miss Eula P. Thompson of Chappel Hill, Washington County. He remained at Clark & Courts for eights years, but grew tired of working there and saw little room for advancement. He then moved to Abilene and turned his attention to the real estate and insurance business. He founded the firm of Will Stith and Company and became a member of the Church of the Heavenly Rest, Episcopal. Stith was also a leader of the Star of the West Lodge Knights of Pythias of Abilene.

In 1921, Stith acquired from W.P. Maffey for the sum of two thousand dollars the property upon which he would eventually build his house four years later. Architect David Castle designed the house in the Tudor-Revival style, including the wood-shingled roof. This style mimics humble medieval cottages and late medieval palaces that may have had overlapping gables, parapets, and beautifully patterned brick or stone work. Traditionally, Tudor-Revival buildings can range from elaborate mansions to modest suburban homes. The Stith House boasts decorative half-timbers, tall narrow windows with small window panes, and a steeply pitched roof. The wood-shingled roof that presents a thatched-like appearance makes the Stith House an architectural highlight in Abilene.

Will Stith lived in the house until his death on April 20, 1930. His widow continued to reside in the house until her death in 1956. Will Stith left his mark on the community of Abilene through his keen business skills and this truly innovative house.

718 Victoria Street

by Tiffany Lynn Grove

The house at 718 Victoria Street has a connection to the Golden Age of Hollywood—almost. Thomas LeSeur, the father of Joan Crawford, worked as a construction laborer on this house. What really makes this home glamorous, however, is not tenuous connections to a movie star, but its reputation as setting the standard in Abilene for its Prairie style architecture of the 1920s.

During the late 1800s and the early 1900s, many cattle families left their ranches and moved to Abilene. One significant rancher who moved to Abilene this period was George R. Davis, a livestock dealer from Breckenridge in Stephens County.

When Davis needed a house built, he chose the renowned architect David Castle to design a beautiful structure. Castle created a Prairie-style model with a covered terrace and balconies in order to bring a touch of the countryside into Davis's new home. To add more to the country flavor, Castle made the dwelling have a sloped roof over the porch and a low pitched hip roof on the second story. Red bricked, squared columns support the first story roof. For construction, Davis chose contractor R.C. Lewis to build the house. The building of the structure totaled $50,000. Mr. Regel was responsible for the house's brickwork. He had red bricks shipped from Pennsylvania to hold up the two-story edifice, and both roofs consist of asphalt shingles. Meanwhile, workers from Fred Gartside Plastering Company provided the plaster work, and Claude Osborne painted the house. In the southwest corner of the house stands the two-story brick garage. Like the house, the garage has equal attention to the country detail.

When Lewis finished building in 1920, the house became known as the best example of the "Prairie School" architecture. Many contractors tried copying the design, but the Davis house reigned as the best in Abilene.

In 1974, Ellis and Opal Goodrum bought the home. The second owners realized that renovations were necessary. So, not only did they repair the house, but they also made sure that it looked just like it did in the 1920s. They wanted to keep it as close to its original form as possible. The structure received many acknowledgements for its beauty. For example, in 1975 the Abilene Board of Realtors honored the house as "a Golden Age Home." Because of this importance, the house was added to the National Historic Register in 1992.

1021 Clinton Street

by Edward Francis De Clements, Jr.

"Click-clack" "click-clack," "ding-ding" "ding-ding." These are the sounds you would have heard around the streets of Abilene in 1908. With the ever-growing population, streetcars started chauffeuring people around town and to the colleges. The Old Streetcar Barn at 1021 Clinton Street is the only visible reminder of those days.

Abilene seemed to be turning into a sprawling community. The visionaries of that time realized the need for some type of public transportation. As early as 1886, business leaders applied for permits to build a streetcar line. It was not to be until 1908, when W.G. Swenson, George Paxton, and J.M. Wagstaff pooled their resources together and developed the Abilene Street Railway Company. In 1908 the company constructed its first building with a wood frame and metal sides. In 1928, the Abilene Street Railway Company built an updated, larger barn at the same location. Constructed with steel framing and metal sides, the building is still in good structural condition and is still used by its current owners as a storage facility.

The Abilene Street Railway Company received its first car from High Point, North Carolina. It was a horse-drawn trolley. Even though Abilene had electricity since 1891, it was not widely used until 1907, when the city built a new power plant. Even though the streetcars were equipped to run on electricity when delivered, it was several years before the streetcar system was completely electric. The company remained in business until absorbed into a new corporation, named Abilene Traction Company. The transition was seamless and did not interrupt transportation. The streetcar ran from Simmons College in north Abilene to what is now Rose Park. It also had a line that ran from the new College Heights addition to the fairgrounds. The Traction Company added a spur line in 1923 to provide service for the newly developed McMurry College.

Throughout the next two decades, the streetcar service was the pride of Abilene. Only the larger cities had such a public transportation system. In 1931, however, a lack of passengers and an increase in automobile ownership led to the company's decision to permanently discontinued streetcar service.

2102 Swenson Street
by Emily Young

The home at 2102 Swenson is known not only for the architectural style in which it was built, but also for its designer. J.G. Higginbotham, a rancher and banker, built this house in 1920. David Castle, a prominent Abilene architect, created the Spanish Mission Colonial Revival style for which the house was built. This style was popular during this time in the West and Southwest.

Spanish Mission Colonial Revival was especially popular between 1900 and 1924. It exemplifies simplicity of form and ornamentation. This is an American style that takes into consideration old colonial styles from England, France, and Spain. The "mission" part of the description defines the simplicity and church-like qualities of the style.

The Higginbotham House stands proud among the other modest homes in the neighborhood. The house includes a large balcony in the center of front façade, with a wrap-around porch, and a two car garage. This house stands as constant reminder for today of a talented architect and of the Texas dream still present in our society.

HENDRICK MEMORIAL HOSPITAL, ABILENE, TEXAS—14

1900 Pine Street

by Brandon Peña

Reverend Millard A. Jenkins, a Baptist minister, was the founding spirit behind Hendrick Hospital. Through his civic and fundraising efforts, the hospital was erected on September 15, 1924, as West Texas Baptist Sanitarium, a Christian Hospital, at the cost of $150,000. The facility originally had five stories with seventy-two rooms, enough to admit more than eight hundred patients in its first year. Each room had hot and cold water. The hospital had three elevators and a well-equipped obstetrical department.

147

The depression of the 1930s left many without proper payment options, so the hospital gladly accepted things ranging from chickens to black-eyed peas. In 1936, T.G. Hendrick, a local oil man, rescued the facility from its troubling financial situation. He provided the hospital with enough money to pay off all debts and build a new wing. Trustees changed the name to Hendrick Memorial Hospital in his honor.

Abilene's growth in the 1940s led to a doubling of the maternity ward to meet with the post-war baby boom. Dyess Air Force Base brought more growth to Abilene in the 1950s. In the 1960s, the hospital added the Anderson Wing, with 84 new rooms, new administrative staff offices, a new clinical lab, and an emergency room. Then they added the Meek Wing in 1966 to house Meek Children's Hospital. The Meek Wing provided much needed additional space for the nursing school, along with a medical library and the blood bank. Since that time, the hospital has added 24-hour Emergency Room service, a Critical Care Unit opened, a Physical Therapy Department, a Patient Relations Department, the Hendrick Center for Rehabilitation, and the Vera West Women's Center. With all of this growth, trustees voted in 1976 to change the name from Hendrick Memorial Hospital to Hendrick Medical Center—a name that honors the past, but also speaks to the continuing evolution of an important Abilene landmark.

Hendrick Memorial Hospital, Abilene, Texas

#59 CALDWELL HALL–HARDIN SIMMONS UNIVERSITY (1922)

2418 Cedar Street

by Kim Smith

Originally dedicated on September 14, 1923, the Caldwell Fine Arts Building on the campus of Hardin-Simmons University houses classrooms, studios, practice rooms, and a recital hall. The historic building is constructed in the architectural style of Beaux Arts/Classical Revival and boasts stained glass skylights, plaster moldings, and Corinthian pilasters atop decorative columns. A beautiful lawn complemented by rose-bushes and ornamental shrubbery surround Caldwell Hall. Paving stones engraved with remembrances purchased by alumni and friends of the School of Music are located in front of the building.

Caldwell Hall is named for "Judge" C.M. Caldwell, who provided funds for its original construction as well as funds in 1959 for an addition and renovations. The building was formally rededicated on September 4, 2003 following a three-year restoration project. The rededication also marked Caldwell Hall's eightieth anniversary.

In 1992, Caldwell Hall was included in the National Registry of Historic Places because it was the site of the first All-Southwest Intercollegiate Piano Tournament. It was also chosen in 2004 for the "Historic Rehabilitation Award" by Preservation Texas, a state-wide partner with the National Trust for Historic Preservation.

435 College Drive

by Kim Smith

Surprisingly nestled in the residential area near Abilene Christian University, the Reese-Thornton House is a three-story English Tudor Cottage with Craftsman influences, surrounded by twenty acres of gardens, wooded paths, orchards, antique rose bushes, and ponds teeming with life. Built by the Reese family in 1924, the 3,500-square-foot house is what appears to be a rural setting in the middle of the city.

In 1941, the E.L. Thornton family bought the property. The Thorntons owned "Thornton's Department Store," so large it was billed as a "City within a City." They lived in the home for fifty-one years, until Bobby and Cindy Deegan bought it in 1992.

The Deegans worked to make improvements on the home and the grounds. They started "Erinshire Gardens," a landscaping company, and they named the home Erinshire, meaning "the green place of peace from whence we derive our strength." The Deegans have converted the carriage house into a bed and breakfast, and in 2003, they started the Erinshire Folk Festival, an annual event that has drawn thousands to the property to enjoy music, food, and the beautiful surroundings. The Deegans sold the house in 2008, and the music festival moved to the grounds of the Buffalo Gap Historic Village in central Taylor County.

1625 Campus Court

by Robert F. Pace

Abilene Christian University got its start in 1906 as the Childers Classical Institute, located on North First Street in Abilene. By 1929, the school had changed its name to Abilene Christian College, and its leaders had made the decision to relocate to much more spacious grounds on the "hill" at the Hashknife Ranch on the northeast side of the city.

An untimely fire in the original administration building on North First, however, hastened the move. Construction crews had to work three shifts to complete the buildings on the new campus in time for the fall 1929 semester to begin. One of the three original buildings constructed was the Sewell Theatre.

College trustees named the building for Jesse P. Sewell and his wife, Daisy. Sewell had served as president of Abilene Christian from 1912 to 1914. The Sewell Theatre played a major role in the new campus development. For most of its existence (1929 to 1968) it served as the location of campus chapel services. In addition, it was the primary location for Abilene Christian's outstanding theater department. Although most theater productions now take place in new Williams Performing Arts Center, the department's Scenic Shop, Costume Shop, and Design Offices are all still housed at the Sewell Theatre.

1755 Campus Court

by Josiah Allen

Abilene Christian University has played an important role in the city of Abilene for more than a hundred years. From its beginning it has served as a focal point in Abilene culture and education. In the mid 1920s, Zona Luce, a successful rancher, donated more than six hundred acres of land to the school. The gift, valued at more than $16,000 was only the second five-figure donation in the school's history. The generosity of this action helped convince school officials to move their campus from its location on North First Street to its current location on the northeast side of Abilene. In 1929, the school named the first of eight buildings constructed at the new site after this generous donor.

This two-story building is constructed in a Classic Renaissance Revival style with a brick veneer. Originally the building housed classrooms for elementary and high school students, the precursor to the creation of Abilene Christian Schools. After nearly seventy years of use, Abilene Christian University began a major renovation campaign for Zona Luce Hall. In 1997 the building, home of the ACU Department of Agriculture and Environment, received a completely new interior and a vastly cleaned exterior. Today, the building looks as good as new and should serve students well into the future.

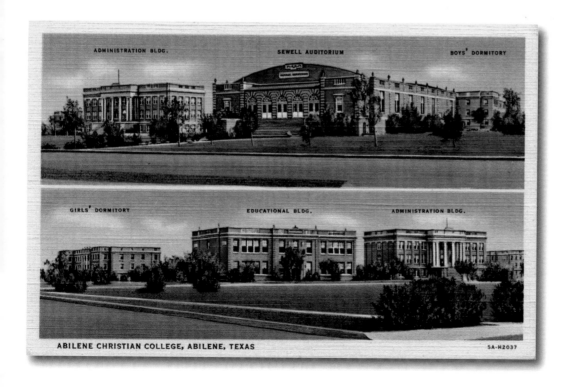

ADMINISTRATION BLDG. SEWELL AUDITORIUM BOYS' DORMITORY

GIRLS' DORMITORY EDUCATIONAL BLDG. ADMINISTRATION BLDG.

ABILENE CHRISTIAN COLLEGE, ABILENE, TEXAS 5A-H2037

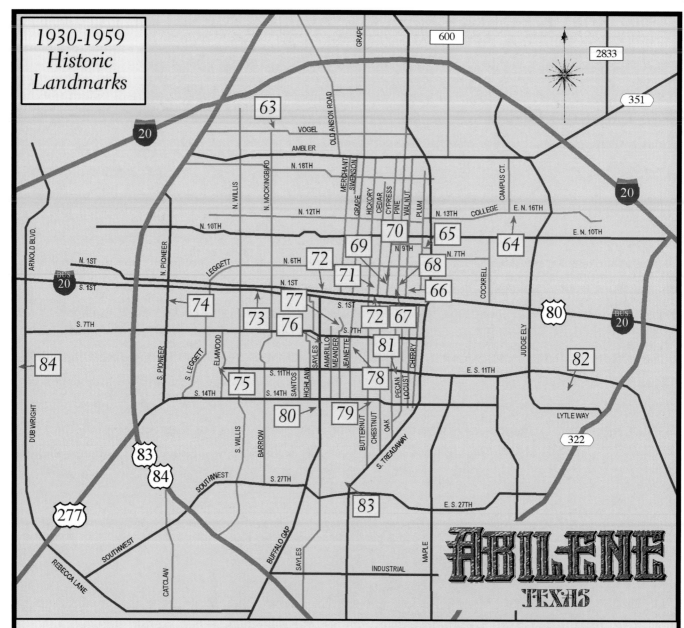

156

1930-1959 Historic Landmarks

ABILENE TEXAS

63. Town & Country Drive-in Theater, 2902 Vogel (1956)
64. University Church of Christ, 733 E.N. 16th (1952)
65. Woodson High School, 520 North 9th (1936)
66. Jordan-Taylor Building, 201 Walnut (1934)
67. McLemore-Bass Building, 216 Pine (1935)
68. Federal Building, 341 Pine (1935)
69. Wooten Hotel, 302 Cypress (1930)
70. Paramount Theater, 352 Cypress (1930)
71. First Baptist Church, 1442 N. 2nd (1954)
72. REA Baggage Bldg. (Candies by Vletas) 1201 N. 1st (1935)
73. Coca-Cola Building, 2074 N. 1st (1951)
74. Borden Milk Company, 309 S. Pioneer (1955)
75. Moreland-Shaheen House, 1120 Elmwood (1946)
76. Frost-Grissom-Moore House, 865 Sayles (1936)
77. Church of the Heavenly Rest, Episcopal, 602 Meander (1954)
78. Sacred Heart Catholic Church, 837 Jeanette (1930)
79. Dixie Pig, 1403 Butternut (1941)
80. Radford Building, McMurry University, 1400 Sayles (1950)
81. Abilene Courts, 633 S. 11th (1930)
82. Shotwell Stadium, 1525 E.S. 11th (1959)
83. Hendrick Home for Children, 2758 Jeanette (1939)
84. Dyess Air Force Base, Dub Wright Blvd. (1956)

TOUR THREE

· ·

1930–1959

While times were tough at the beginning of this era, Abilene added some of its most enduring and endearing landmarks during this thirty-year period of record growth. After a depressing decade of economic hardship, Abilene did its share to help the United States win World War II. Camp Barkeley introduced the community to the joys of hosting a military installation, and thousands of soldiers flooded the streets of Abilene, mingling with thousands of new residents who came to town to take advantage of wartime jobs and opportunities. Even though the local economy began its shift from being a shipping hub for agricultural commodities to new ways of making money, the postwar boom continued rolling, and the city tripled in population while gaining an important new landmark: Dyess Air Force Base.

157

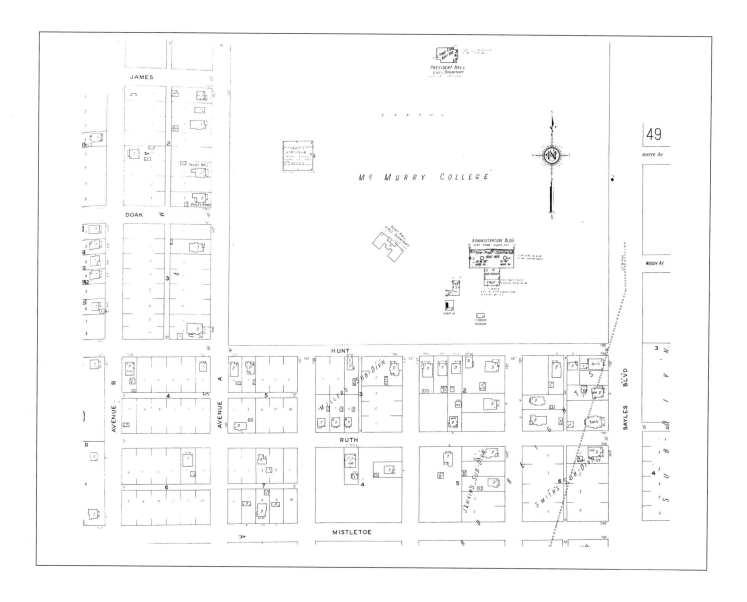

2902 Vogel Street

by Kristina Green

At the height of the American "Drive-In Era," Texas housed the most, boasting more than four hundred drive-ins theaters. By the time the Town and Country Drive-in opened, Abilene already contained six others. The Town and Country Drive-in Theater distinguished itself due to its sheer size, claiming to be the biggest screen in Abilene. It opened on July 21, 1956, with *Guys and Dolls* and remained open for twenty-five years before closing on September 10, 1981.

The theater remained closed for nineteen years, during which time all of the other drive-in theaters in Abilene also shut down. This occurrence simply matched the trend nationwide, as 96% of all drive-in theaters built in the twentieth century are no longer in business today. On July 7, 2000, two theater enthusiasts reopened the Town and Country Drive-in with the movie, *Dinosaurs*. Since then, they have brought back the tradition of the drive-in theater and the use of the double-feature. The Town and Country Drive-in is truly a landmark reminiscent of its decade of origin, the 1950s.

159

733 East North Sixteenth Street

by Terann Ragland

161

University Church of Christ congregation in Abilene has always been closely connected to what is now known as Abilene Christian University. The predecessor to the university, Childers Classical Institute, got its start on North First Street in 1906. With this beginning of the college, the infant congregation began meeting in the administration building of the school, calling itself the College Church of Christ. In 1929, Abilene Christian College moved to the north side of town. Some members of the congregation remained near the location of the original college and formed the Highland Church of Christ. The rest, however, moved with the college, meeting in various locations over the years, until finally building the current structure at 733 E. N. Sixteenth in 1952.

The first service in the new building took place on February 10. Over the years, the congregation has made several additions to the structure, including an Education Wing in 1960 and an activity center in 1978. A Rainbow Bible School began in 1979 as a school meeting two days a week. Since then the school has developed into a five-day a week school, which demonstrated the need for the building of the Early Childhood Center in 1988. The deep roots of the University Church of Christ, dating back to the early twentieth century, have helped to mold the society of Abilene in many ways.

520 North Ninth Street

by Edward Francis De Clements, Jr.

Some landmarks are important because they remind a society of its past sins. Vestiges of our country's segregation laws fall into this category. However, we can also learn great lessons of hope and strength from those who endured through these trying times. African Americans have been a part of Abilene's history from the very beginning. And despite the problems of Jim Crow, they have been able to find ways to contribute.

According to the city census, there were eleven black children living in Abilene in 1885. It was not until 1890, however, that some kind of educational facility was available to them. Then, African American parents decided to hire a teacher, who taught twenty-two black students at the Mount Zion Baptist Church. This was a one-room building located on Plum Street.

In 1902 the Abilene School district built a new College Heights School, moved the old one-room school building to North Seventh and Treadaway, and made it Abilene's first official "Colored School." The building space provided room for the eighty-two pupils and two teachers. This action started the school's "hand-me-down" supply system. Dorothy Wiseman, a 1946 Woodson School graduate and educator, asserted, "We were in a sense like the prospective new bride except already had something old, we wanted something new, they gave us something borrowed and for the most part, we were blue. We were in fact, little Cinderellas—we got all the cast offs, all the hand-me-downs." Through the years, Abilene's Colored School received all of its books, desks, and athletic equipment used from the white schools that had received new materials and equipment.

Finally, in 1936, construction of a new ten-room brick all-grades black school began. The Carter G. Woodson School is located at 520 North Ninth Street. This was the first time the black school received anything new. By 1952, the growth in the student population required the district to build a new black school, which they named the Carter G. Woodson Junior-Senior High School. They renamed the 1936 facility Woodson Elementary School. Woodson High School remained segregated until 1969—fifteen years after the celebrated Supreme Court case, *Brown v. Board of Education of Topeka, Kansas*, which ruled segregation to be unconstitutional. Woodson closed after the completion of desegregation.

Even through all its hardships and transitions, the Woodson Schools are still in use today. The original—on 9th Street—houses the Abilene Independent School District's Early Childhood Program.

201 Walnut Street

by Michael Jerry Akin

Success in the furniture business is always risky, but the building at 201 Walnut Street has been lucky for furniture business owners for multiple decades. The building's brick and mortar framed style is classic, and the front solid-wooden doors add character and charm and display the craftsmanship of its time. Large glass windows are located on two sides of the building allowing a view of the furniture displayed inside the store.

Success first came to this building in 1934 when Waldrop's Furniture, which had been established by Gideon Waldrop in 1923, moved from its original location at 220 Cypress Street. Gideon and Margaret had three children, two boys and one girl. After a five-year job with the FBI, Gideon's youngest son, Alfred Sam Waldrop became a partner in his father's business in 1946. Sam took over as president of company upon his father's death in 1968.

"Better Homes Within Reach of All," reads a Waldrop's advertisement in the 1928 phone directory. When asked about this ad before his own death in 2007, Sam Waldrop expressed satisfaction with the sentiment, proclaiming, "the ad is simple, yet effective." He elaborated: "reputation was and still is the key to success." Even though the store generated two to three million dollars annually in sales by 2004, Sam Waldrop decided to retire, and he closed down the business.

Within the next year, however, Jordan Taylor and Company, a fine furniture store that had begun in 1999, moved into the site. With this addition, 201 Walnut should provide Abileneans with fine furniture for decades more to come.

216 Pine Street

by Sara Ritson

The McLemore-Bass Drug Company opened its doors to customers in 1935 at 216 Pine Street. Two partners, A.T. McLemore and Henry J. Bass, ran the store. Their mission was to sell drugs and serums that were needed for pneumonia, snakebites, and other ailments. After 1975 the property no longer contained a drug store. It did, however, hold many other businesses, such as Buddy's Shoe Clinic and Texas Blue Print Company.

In 1991, the building was renovated and reopened. One of the new businesses to open was the Green Frog, a live music entertainment spot. In 2001 the Green Frog closed its doors. New owners turned the building into an Italian restaurant, Spano's Trattoria. When the store was renovated, it was designed to look just as it did when the drug store was located in the building. In 2007, Alley Cats Restaurant took over the space. The McLemore-Bass building is listed on the National Register of Historic Places among all the other fascinating buildings that are located in Abilene.

168

A 1950s photo postcard showing the old post office building to the right and the Federal Building to the left, and the old Hilton Hotel, renamed the Windsor, in the background.

341 Pine Street

by Kim Smith

The current United States Post Office and Federal Courthouse, located at the corner of North Third and Pine Streets, was constructed in 1935. The architectural firm used for the job was Abilene's own David S. Castle Company, with supervising architect Louis A Simon leading the design. Simon created the building in the architectural style known as Art Deco, a popular American design style between 1925 and 1949.

With one addition made to the original structure in 1963, the building now serves as the Federal Courthouse, United States Post Office, Internal Revenue Service, and probation offices. It was added to the National Register of Historical Places in 1992.

West Texas Chamber of Commerce and Museum
Abilene, Texas

Landmarks lost, this postcard reveals the old post office building on North Third and the spacious park and gazebo between it and the Hilton Hotel beyond. The building was already adapted for other purposes as indicated by the caption. All of this open space now lies beneath the Federal Building complex.

U.S. POST OFFICE AND COURT HOUSE, ABILENE, TEXAS.

Hotel Wooten, Abilene, Texas

CYPRESS STREET LOOKING SOUTH, ABILENE, TEXAS—15

302 Cypress Street

by Leah Herod

The Wooten Hotel is a well-known landmark, as it remains one of the oldest, most impressive buildings in Abilene. The Wooten Hotel maintains a certain symbolic value, which is helpful in preserving Abilene's historic community. The hotel, built by H.O. Wooten, was financed under what many would consider to be surprising circumstances—its construction was paid for entirely in cash. Wooten worked in the wholesale grocery business, but it was his oil investments in West Texas that supplied him the cash for the construction of the hotel. Hoping that it would provide Abilene a luxurious hotel and help promote culture, H.O. Wooten began construction of this structure in 1927.

The million-dollar hotel opened on June 6, 1930, with a celebration that lasted all weekend. Fashioned after the Drake Hotel in Chicago, the Wooten strived to capture grandeur of its northern cousin. The Wooten featured a ballroom, mezzanine, lobby, dining room, banquet hall, penthouse, mens' club, and ladies' lounge. Some considered Wooten to be the most elite hotel between Fort Worth and El Paso. Wooten even provided silver flatware for the finest of dining. The third floor club was said to be comparable to one found in upscale hotels in Manhattan, with membership limited at 150. Wooten's attractions continued to attract visitors as it provided a gymnasium, apparatus room, card room, game room, and roof garden.

By West Texas standards, some considered the sixteen-story hotel to be a genuine skyscraper. The display of luxury was captured by architect David S. Castle and E.V. McCright the general contractor. Castle designed the façade to introduce Abilene to the art deco style. Wooten has light-tan brick detailed with cast-stone panels. Arched windows line the bottom as well as the top of Wooten's tower. Not only was style considered, but fire prevention was also an important part in the designing of the hotel.

After World War II, the Wooten experienced hard times. The Wooten family sold the hotel in 1959 to E.L.T. Inc., but it returned to them two years later. In 1963 West Texas Residential Center Inc., which consisted of local residents, obtained the building. This group completely renovated the structure, adding air conditioning and a 160-car garage. The hotel became housing for senior citizens. In 1965, with low occupancy, the Wooten was a financial drain. California developer Paul Oman purchased the property. After owning the building for twenty-five years, it was in shambles. In 1998 Bill Wenson bought the Wooten with the idea of turning it into apartments targeting young professionals. Tony Eeds was selected to provide historic restoration of the building, and the building reopened in 2004 with much of its original splendor restored. Once again, Abilene can embrace the Wooten as an enduring symbol of pride.

352 Cypress Street

by Crissi Renaye Reneau

The Paramount Theatre was built in 1930 and was the largest theatre in town. David Castle, a local architect, designed the building. In 1928 Horace Wooten—a grocery wholesaler, real estate investor, and oilman—financed the construction of the Paramount Theatre to complement the Wooten Hotel, which he was building next door. He paid $400,000 in cash to have the theatre built. The theatre's main design is to reflect a Spanish/Moorish architecture.

On May 19, 1930, the Paramount opened its doors to the public and successfully had a sold out show. More than five thousand people turned out to the first show. The theatre could seat 1,500 people and cost forty to sixty cents for adults and fifteen cents for children.

The Paramount was the brightest place in town with the help of the beautifully constructed ninety-foot marquee that held around 1,400 light bulbs. At the Paramount, Abilenians entered into another domain, mesmerized by the big, white, puffy clouds and twinkling stars projected on the ceiling, giving the appearance of a perfect summer night.

In 1986 the Paramount was restored to its original grandeur. The structure now has the technology to present live theatre, classic films, modern movies, art films, animation videos, concerts, worship ceremonies, parties, business gatherings, and weddings. This landmark is a true jewel among Abilene's buildings.

An interior shot of the restored Paramount Theater showing the Spanish inspired details all around, the simulated night sky above, and a house full of paying customers.

1442 North Second Street

By KC Walters

Dr. O.C. Pope was on a mission in the late 1800s to start as many Baptist churches as possible in West Texas; as a result First Baptist Church of Abilene was founded in 1881.

The church went through several buildings before settling in the current structure. The first church building, built in 1883, stood on the corner of North Fourth Street and Cedar. The congregation soon outgrew this small clapboard building and built a larger structure in 1909 on the corner of North Second Street and Hickory at the cost of $56,000. The building was the largest in Abilene at the time and shared by the whole community. By the late 1940s the building, worn beyond repair, had become too small for the growing congregation. Plans for the current building began in 1950.

The pastor who oversaw the planning of this building was Dr. Jesse Northcutt. The congregation appointed a committee of five to discuss the plans, and they in turn appointed an even bigger committee. Members of the Heavenly Rest Episcopal Church at North Third Street and Orange agreed also wanted to build a larger building, so they sold their lot to the Baptists and moved to a neighborhood south of downtown. This purchase gave First Baptist Church room to build. Construction commenced and the new building opened in 1954 at a cost of nearly $1.2 million.

It took 325 tons of steel to raise the building, including the spire, which rises 140 feet from the ground. The architect and engineers were the F.C. Olds Company and the Contractor was Rose Construction Company. The committee, pastor, architect, and contractor worked closely to draw up the plans of this Romanesque building, modeled after churches all over the country. The architects visited several of these churches personally in the hopes of creating a unique style of their own. The plan was a success. Elwin Skiles was the pastor during the completion of the church in February 1954. He held a weeklong dedication revival, celebrating the opening of the new church.

In 2006, the church unveiled yet another major renovation to the auditorium. This improvement included new carpet and new wiring to accommodate the high tech sound system and video system. The balcony was also reshaped to improve acoustics. The building stands as a testament to hard work and a dedicated congregation.

A tired and rundown Railroad Express Agency building long before its present-day "sweetening."

1201 North First Street

by Carlos V. Montez

For Americans at the beginning of the twentieth century to send a large package or crate a long distance, it depended on which "express" company had agreements with the railroad company in their town. In 1917, however, the United States government nationalized several of these express companies, then a decade later, sold the new entity to the railroads. In 1929, this new company took on the name "Railway Express Agency."

By the 1930s Americans knew the Railway Express Agency as the REA, and they came to rely on the carrier to be able to deliver their packages and cargo across the country in a timely manner. In cities and towns throughout the nation, REA baggage depots sprung up to handle the large volume of cargo shipped on these special trains.

Abilene's REA Baggage Building was constructed in 1935 and has many characteristics common to its fellow REA buildings. It is an excellent example of a twentieth-century commercial railroad structure. Some of the features include the metal hip roof, which is wide and overhung. The roof is supported by unadorned brackets. It has double wood doors with diamond-patterned transoms. Transoms are usually horizontal crosspieces over a door or between doors, a motif repeated on the windows in the structure.

In 1997 the REA Baggage Building became the third of the old railroad buildings in Abilene to undergo total restoration. The city's Tax Increment Financing District Board backed spending $523,550 to renovate the building. In 1999, long-time Abilene specialty confectioner, Candies by Vletas, moved into the depot, bringing the old structure a new, sweet-smelling life.

177

2074 North First Street

by Kristina Green

At the beginning of the twentieth century, J.W. Childers owned a house and the surrounding land at 2074 North First Street. In 1906 A. B. Barrett proposed to build an institution of higher learning affiliated with the Church of Christ. Childers sold Barrett the land and the house on the property at a reduced rate with the understanding that the school would be named in his honor. On September 11, 1906, Barrett and Charles Roberson founded the Childers Classical Institute with twenty-five students. Within a decade, the school began using the name Abilene Christian College. In 1927, the city of Abilene assisted the college in the purchase of new land, and in 1929 the college vacated its original campus, leaving a few dormitories and a gymnasium behind.

Shortly thereafter, Coca-Cola of Texas moved its bottling operation into the old A.C.C. gym. Eventually, the dormitory at North First and Graham became the administrative offices for Coca-Cola. Throughout the 1930s and '40s, Coca-Cola operated out of these buildings on this site. In 1951, they built the building that now stands at 2074 North First. The structure had a large second-floor meeting room that became popular for meetings of many civic groups through the 1950s and '60s. The building continued to be the Abilene headquarters for Coca-Cola until the early 1990s. After remaining vacant for several years, Higginbotham Brothers Lumber Yard took over the space. Then in 2007 Global Samaritans, a non-profit outreach organization, moved into the building. For more than a century now, this piece of real estate has been an important Abilene landmark.

179

309 South Pioneer Drive

by Gail Adlesperger

Gail Borden, Jr., founded the New York Condensed Milk Company, built upon his process of creating condensed milk, which could be shipped long distances without cooling. In 1919, the company was renamed the Borden Company, and throughout the next couple of decades, the organization bought more than two hundred dairy companies around the country, making it the largest seller of fluid milk in the nation. Abilene was one of those new markets for Borden Milk.

Looking at the classic Colonial style architecture of the Borden Milk Company at 309 S. Pioneer Drive, one can see back to the early days of the Borden Company. This building was constructed in 1955 to be a replica of the original Borden Milk Plant. Originally painted pale pink and white, it is now only white. The two-story Colonial style building has large front columns. This building is now a distribution office for the Borden Milk Company in this area, not a manufacturing facility.

1120 Elmwood Drive

by Leah Herod

Among the many beautiful homes on Elmwood Drive, one in particular stands out –the Moreland-Shaheen House at 1120 Elmwood. Recognized by its striking style, and affectionately nicknamed the "Sugar House," this landmark serves as a reminder of the help many Abilenians received during World War II.

While sugar was almost impossible to obtain during and immediately after World War II, Henry J. Moreland and his wife Bernice provided this sweet staple to other Abilenians. Since Moreland operated the city's Dr. Pepper and 7-Up bottling companies, he had a steady supply of sugar from the government. He sold much of his allotment directly to Abilenians who wanted this scarce resource. The Morelands used the proceeds from their sugar sales and built this estate on Elmwood.

Designed by a local architectural and engineering firm, Hughes & Olds, the house boasts a solid construction of Austin stone, supported with concrete steal beams. Built in 1946 the home is a replica of actress Joan Crawford's mansion in Hollywood. From the 1920s to the 1940s, the Art Modern style found in the Sugar House architecture was popular in Hollywood. This style can be recognized by the abundance of chrome, mirrors, and tile glass used in the architecture, as well as horizontal lines with long simple repeated curved lines.

Featured nationally in 1946, the property remains truly unique. The estate has a variety of trees including apple, apricot, pear, persimmon, pomegranate, and pecan. Stone entrances tower over built on each side of the property, along with a circular drive in the back. A spacious circular screened patio, Austin stone barbecue pit, water well, as well as a separate two-car garage with a servant's quarters can also be found at the back of the property.

Unaltered over the years, the inside is decorated with sculpted moldings and ceiling medallions, in addition to birds-eye maple wood trim. The Sugar House is a complete package of luxury including a wine cellar, garden room that features a waterfall with rocks collected by Bernice Moreland, and a round sunbath on the second floor. Also featured is a large staircase with a curving chrome-banister, a chandelier, and elaborately etched sliding glass doors. The extraordinary dining room displays outstanding chandeliers and is complete with moldings and mirrors that open for food serving.

The Sugar House also provides a three level basement, projection room and a bomb shelter. At the start of the Cold War the city designated this basement as a bomb shelter for about five hundred people in case of an air raid. The home has now stood majestically alongside many lovely residences on Elmwood, but none of them are quite as sweet as the Sugar House.

865 Sayles Boulevard

by Ben Hoyng

The Frost/Grissom/Moore House at 865 Sayles Boulevard is one of the larger homes in the Sayles Boulevard Historic District. This prestigious property has a popular architectural style from the early twentieth century, the Spanish Colonial Revival. The building exemplifies the history of Abilene during the early twentieth century through this unique architecture. There are the intricate details of the home such as the statues posing in the front yard, the half-circle driveway, the stonework in the walls, as well as the detailed molding and ironwork. Built in 1936 the home still remains intact, but has undergone significant many renovations and updates over the years.

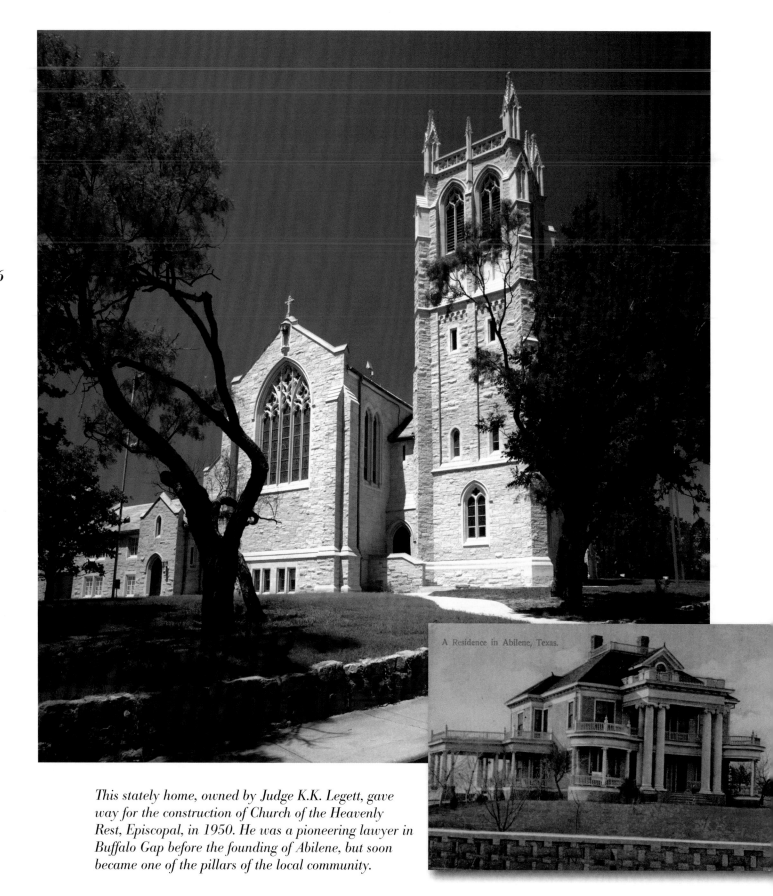

A Residence in Abilene, Texas.

This stately home, owned by Judge K.K. Legett, gave way for the construction of Church of the Heavenly Rest, Episcopal, in 1950. He was a pioneering lawyer in Buffalo Gap before the founding of Abilene, but soon became one of the pillars of the local community.

602 Meander Street

by Jim Jarrett

"PAX VOBISCUM: Friend, you have come to this church, leave it not without a prayer. No man entering a house ignores him who dwells in it. This is the house of God and He is here." These words grace a plaque just inside the northeast entrance of the Church of the Heavenly Rest, Abilene's very own English Country Gothic Church, and one of the few examples of churches designed in the authentic gothic architecture style built west of the Mississippi River. Rising majestically above a quiet neighborhood in southeast Abilene, the Church of the Heavenly Rest is the oldest Episcopal Church in the city. It has not, however, always been located at South Sixth Street and Meander.

The original location was at North Third and Orange Streets. Completed in 1884, the church was built of native stone and was the only building constructed of permanent material in the town for nearly twenty-five years. Due to steady growth, the parish had outgrown the building by 1949. The church bought the lot at South Sixth and Meander Streets for $25,000.00.

The Reverend Willis Gerhart became the Rector of the Church of the Heavenly Rest in February 1920. He served for the next thirty-eight years. When the church needed to expand, Parson Gerhart, as he came to be called, pushed for the building of a true gothic church. The plan to build at the new site was approved, and the renowned architect Philip Frohman was hired to design the structure. Frohman was one of the two architects who designed the National Cathedral in Washington, D.C. He told Gerhart he wanted to design the type of church that one would find in a typical English country village. Frohman's design was finalized and companies were asked for bids on the project. None were received. Construction companies in Abilene had no experience building gothic structures, and were understandably afraid to try. Finally, Rose and Son Company agreed to build the structures. In 1951 the congregation moved from the original site to a surplus army Quonset hut in which to conduct services and began construction.

The Parish House was the first building completed. It houses the Sunday school rooms. It was also the original site for St. John's Episcopal School. The last building completed was the Parish Hall, in 1971. This building is the fellowship area of the church. In between the completion of these two structures, was the construction of the church itself.

The nave is the only part that is completely Gothic. Like the other buildings, the nave is built of Lueders limestone. The walls are four feet thick ant the base, tapering to two and a half feet at the top. The congregation first used the nave on Easter Sunday, 1956. At the time, there were no windows, pews, or roof. The nave was completed in November 1956. The final portion of construction was that of the Bell Tower, finished in 1981. Construction took twenty-eight years to complete the structure, but to all who look upon the beautiful Gothic church, it was worth the wait.

CATHOLIC SACRED HEART CHURCH AND RECTORY, ABILENE, TEXAS—17

837 Jeanette Street

by Mandy Elson

In 1881, shortly after the founding of the city of Abilene, Catholic occupants of the new city cried out for a parish to call their own. Even when tents made up most of the structures in the infant town, Father Henry David Brickley began visiting Abilene regularly on the third Sunday of each month. From these humble beginnings, the presence of Catholicism in Abilene would eventually lead to the establishment of the Sacred Heart Catholic Church.

In 1891, Father Brickley set about constructing a church for the Catholic congregation. He raised money through bazaars and even recruited neighboring Protestants to help build the church. On September 9, 1892, the first Sacred Heart Catholic Church of Abilene was opened and servicing the community. From 1892 to 1919, this building served the local Catholic congregation, but soon the church was too small to house the growing population. Also, the original church was too far from St. Joseph's Academy, which was located near South Ninth and Amarillo Street.

A new priest, Father Henry Knufer, recognized this problem and sought aid to help build a larger church. On April 29, 1926, the congregation selected a site on the corner of South Eighth and Jeanette Streets and bought it for the cost of $2, 500. They raised money through pledge drives and loans as the acting bishop gave permission to build a new church. The architect was Leo Dielman, of San Antonio, who had designed many Catholic churches. Father Knufer wanted a impressive building to compete with the large buildings of the local Protestant colleges. Balfanz Construction Company built the new church at the approximate cost of $55,000. The Sacred Heart Catholic Church is a large brick structure with a corner bell tower that was influenced heavily by Romanesque architecture. There are many aspects of Romanesque architecture that are featured in the Sacred Heart Catholic Church. The nave is higher and narrower to make room for windows, the openings are small and decorated with moldings, carvings, and sculptures, and the doors and windows are capped by round arches.

Although the building was mostly complete by the end of 1930, the first Mass in the finished church took place on Holy Thursday, April 2, 1931. The doors where officially opened on Easter Sunday, April 5, 1931. The church has continued to project majestic beauty as stained glass windows and air conditioning were added in the 1950s. The church still has an active, vibrant congregation, and it is an important landmark to Abilene's past and future.

1403 Butternut Street

by Kristina Green

The Dixie Pig Restaurant opened in 1931 on the corner of South 14th and Butternut streets. In 1941, however, the building was torn down and replaced with the structure that still stands today at the busy intersection. As a reflection of the changing times, the new facility included a car-hop feature. The diner hosted locals new to town who were moving into the growing neighborhoods in the area, as well as college students and faculty from nearby McMurry and even soldiers on weekend passes from Camp Barkeley.

Business was good. The north dining room was added in 1948, replacing what used to be a car-hop area. The brick building has always been painted white, but it originally had red trim. At some point, the trim was painted green, and in 1986, owners painted it blue. The restaurant specializes in breakfast and lunch, and is usually crowded, as it has been for decades.

191

A colorful 1950s postcard view of the famous Dixie Pig, looking southeast from the corner of Butternut and South Fourteenth. This was during the restaurant's "red" phase.

192

RADFORD STUDENT CENTER, MCMURRY COLLEGE, ABILENE, TEXAS

MCMURRY UNIVERSITY

#80 RADFORD BUILDING, MCMURRY UNIVERSITY (1950)

1400 Sayles Boulevard

by Joseph Trey Cox III

One of the most visible landmarks on Sayles Boulevard is the beautiful Radford Building of McMurry University. Built in 1950, the structure serves as the ceremonial center of the campus, providing the venue for decades of convocation and commencement ceremonies, in addition to thousands of other day-to-day uses. It also occupies one of the highest points in the Abilene city limits, making its spire visible from most parts of town.

In 1947, Mrs. J.M. Radford donated $300,000 to be used in building an auditorium, student social center, and the attached library capable of holding 100,000 texts. With the rising costs of postwar inflation Mrs. Radford's donation was insufficient. President Harold G. Cooke made many proposals to the Board of Trustees, but nothing developed. In 1949, Mrs. Radford made another donation of $300,000 allowing the school to build the structure, but without a proposed library wing. Recreational facilities would be in the basement, and lounges and parlors would be on the first and second floors of the west side of the building.

The attitude at the dedication ceremony of Radford Memorial Building in 1950 was a joyous one. Many alumni reunited and had a time of celebration in the shadow of the newest building on campus. In the summer of 1958, the Student Union Building (SUB), post office, and bookstore were moved to the south end of Radford. In 1963, Mrs. Alleese Wood donated funds to air condition the building. The annual homecoming musical, university chapel services, and major community activities still take place in the Radford Auditorium.

In 2000 the building received a million dollar renovation, creating office space for the university Financial Aid and Admissions Departments. In 2007, the university completed construction of the Bedford and Oneta Furr Welcome Center, attached to the south side of the Radford Building and providing handicapped-accessible restroom facilities for the Radford Auditorium. It is clear that the graceful Radford Building will remain an Abilene landmark for decades more to come, and continues to serve as the heart of McMurry.

633 South Eleventh Street

by Malaney Lopez

195

In 1926, the American Association of State Highway Officials adopted a plan to have numbered highways cross the country. Out of this plan, US Highway 80 was born. Also known as the Dixie Overland Highway, US 80 traversed the southern portion of the United States, from Savannah, Georgia, to San Diego, California. This highway went straight through the middle of Abilene, incorporating many parts of the decade-old Bankhead Highway along the way.

As more and more motorists hit the road traveling on the numbered highways, the "motor court" was born as the predominant type of lodging for these travelers. Combining the convenience of an interior court for parking and easily accessible rooms or cabins, the motor court became favored by many motorists over the traditional hotel with a lobby.

The Abilene Courts, located on South Eleventh, were built in 1930 alongside the famous Highway 80. Once the interstate system came into being, most towns and cities were bypassed, making the motor courts along the old highways less needed. Now abandoned, the Abilene Courts still stand as a reminder of the once-popular stop on Highway 80, and is the direct ancestor of motels (motor + hotels) that line America's interstates today.

1525 East South Eleventh Street

by Jennifer Wells

Football is deeply rooted in the heart of Texas cultural. In 1959, Abilene's Shotwell Stadium opened, modeled after the Rice University Stadium, and located at 1525 E.S. Eleventh Street. Shotwell Stadium hosted its first game in the fall 1959 under the name, Public Schools Stadium. After the first season legendary Abilene High School football coach P.E. "Pete" Shotwell donated his name to the facility. The stadium seats 15,046 fans and serves as the home field for Abilene Christian University, Cooper High School, and Abilene High School.

In the mid 1970s, Shotwell Stadium witnessed a feat that has never been beaten at any level of football play before or since. On October 16, 1976, Abilene Christian University player Ove Johansson kicked a 69-yard field goal against East Texas State University.

In 2002, Abilene Independent School District made major upgrades including Safe-Play turf, new goal posts, and a new drainage system among others. In 2003, two new scoreboards were placed at the north and south end of the stadium, making it one of the select few in Texas to boast two boards. A brand new 34-foot-tall scoreboard equipped with a 14' by 24' high definition video screen replaced the four-year-old north end scoreboard. This state-of-the-art screen rivals any other high school scoreboard in the country and allows for instant replays, commercials, and more.

2758 Jeanette Street

by Anders Jordan Leverton

Thomas G. and Ida Nations Hendrick established the Hendrick Home for Children in 1939, after Joseph, their four-year-old son, passed away. From that experience, the couple devoted their lives to passionately caring for all children.

In 1939 this establishment originally consisted of the main four-story complex, and three staff houses located behind it, and they were not built cheaply. At the time, Hendrick Home for Children had the best of the best. They had an indoor theatre with a seating capacity for three hundred, a stainless steel kitchen, a basement with a barber shop, beauty salon, three huge refrigerators for storage, and dentist's and doctor's offices for their on-staff doctors, a barn, and even an infirmary located on the third level. Essentially, these components of the building made it into its own private city. Over the year, other improvements came to the site. In the 1970s the school added a full-size gymnasium and swimming pool, followed later by baseball fields with batting cages.

Despite the luxuries, one of the main goals of Hendrick Home is to teach the children to live productive lives. All children had to perform chores, including laundry, ironing, milking cows and collecting eggs.

As times changed, so did Hendrick Home. The children now live in smaller homes throughout the complex with "house parents." The main building serves as the gathering place and administrative offices. The two-story theatre is still there. The top level or balcony had been a library, and is now offices for their compassionate staff. The theatre is still present in its original condition, with its 1940s-light style and pulley system on the proscenium-style stage, and serves many purposes. The facility is still composed of its original thick concrete walls, lights, exit signs, and floors. Commitment and compassion at this level makes Hendrick Home, as the name implies, a home.

200

Eighteen B-1s and seven C-130s are visible in this view, demonstrating the importance of Dyess Air Force Base to the national security of the United States.

A replica of the P-40 Warhawk fighter flown by Colonel William Dyess in the 1941-1942 Philippine Campaign against the Japanese stands outside the air force base named in his honor. He called his plane Kibosh, a slang term for putting a stop to contrary behavior. This Albany native "put the kibosh" on the enemy during World War II as often as he could.

Dub Wright Boulevard

by Jennifer Wells

In World War II, the Abilene area had a significant contribution to the war effort, hosting not only Camp Barkeley, but also the nearby Tye Army Air Field. Once the war ended, both sites were decommissioned. Abilene city leaders, however, wanted to see the return of a major military base to the city to help the local economy and to play a role in national security. In the Cold War era, the government was looking for locations to put long-range bomber bases. When Abilene raised one million dollars to purchase land adjacent to the old Tye Army Air Field, Washington took notice and named Abilene the site of the new base.

Initially the base was to be called the Abilene Air Force Base, shortly after it opened in 1956, it became Dyess, named after Albany, Texas, native Lt. Col. William E. Dyess. An aviation enthusiast since watching barnstormers cross the West Texas skies in the 1920s, Dyess joined the army to learn to fly. At the outbreak of World War II he was piloting a P-40 Warhawk in air sorties against the Japanese invasion of the Philippines. Eventually, he and the other airmen ran out of bases and equipment as the Japanese continued their conquest, and Dyess led an ad hoc force of pilots and ground crews as a stopgap infantry command. Captured along with the balance of U.S. forces in the Philippines, he survived the Bataan Death March only to languish for months under extreme conditions in a prisoner of war pen.

Dyess escaped, joined a band of Filipino guerillas, and harassed the Japanese occupiers until finally making it back to American lines. After returning to the U.S. and recuperating, he sought a return to active combat duty even though he could have taken a safer assignment. While Dyess was flying a training mission in a P-38, his aircraft caught fire. Instead of jumping to safety and crashing his plane in a heavily populated area, Dyess remained at the controls of the stricken craft and brought the plane down in a vacant lot, losing his life in the effort. Today the base that bears his name hosts the 7th Bomb Wing, and plays an active part in military operations around the globe. Its B-1 Lancer bombers and C-130 Hercules transport aircraft are common fixtures in the Abilene sky.

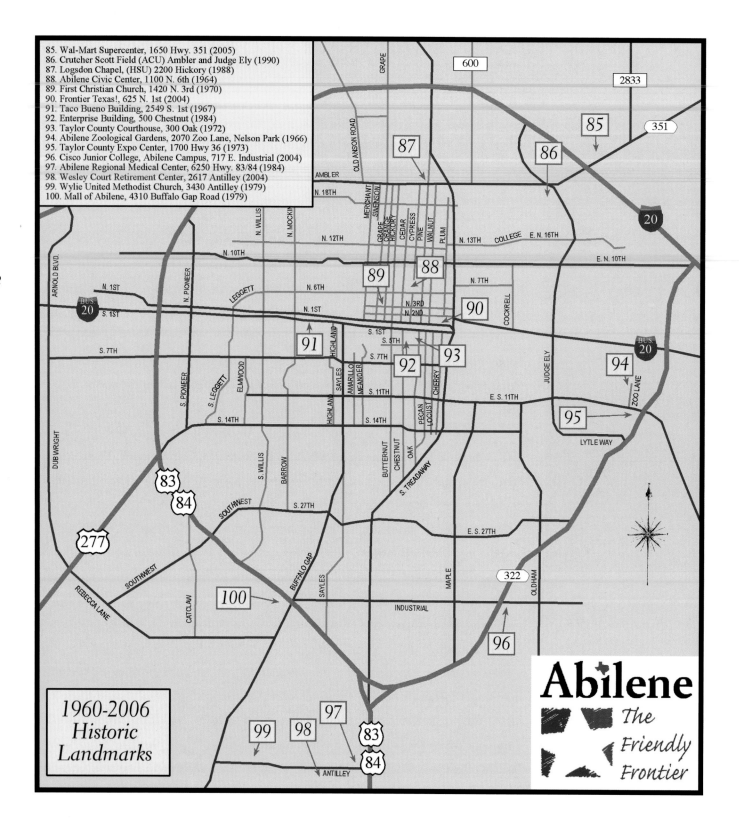

85. Wal-Mart Supercenter, 1650 Hwy. 351 (2005)
86. Crutcher Scott Field (ACU) Ambler and Judge Ely (1990)
87. Logsdon Chapel, (HSU) 2200 Hickory (1988)
88. Abilene Civic Center, 1100 N. 6th (1964)
89. First Christian Church, 1420 N. 3rd (1970)
90. Frontier Texas!, 625 N. 1st (2004)
91. Taco Bueno Building, 2549 S. 1st (1967)
92. Enterprise Building, 500 Chestnut (1984)
93. Taylor County Courthouse, 300 Oak (1972)
94. Abilene Zoological Gardens, 2070 Zoo Lane, Nelson Park (1966)
95. Taylor County Expo Center, 1700 Hwy 36 (1973)
96. Cisco Junior College, Abilene Campus, 717 E. Industrial (2004)
97. Abilene Regional Medical Center, 6250 Hwy. 83/84 (1984)
98. Wesley Court Retirement Center, 2617 Antilley (2004)
99. Wylie United Methodist Church, 3430 Antilley (1979)
100. Mall of Abilene, 4310 Buffalo Gap Road (1979)

202

1960-2006
Historic
Landmarks

Abilene
The
Friendly
Frontier

TOUR FOUR

1960–2006

Nearly eighty years after its founding, Abilene had reached a developmental crossroads. The modern era broke upon the city in interesting ways that played out among its homes and businesses, its residents and visitors. New styles of buildings climbed skyward at the same time as the area economy became more oriented toward banking, commerce, and retail. A galloping oil boom brought new faces to town and realigned the way the city grew as new fortunes vied with old money for a stake in the destiny of the community. Before long, highways ringed Abilene, which had spread out all over the prairie. Instead of recycling older real estate like it had in the past, Abilene pushed out its city limits in all directions, especially to the south. With a downtown in danger of dying as the commercial energy migrated to the edge of town, only the concerted efforts and infusion of capital by its citizens saved Abilene from becoming a developmental and cultural donut, the unintended victim of natural economic forces that marked these times all across the nation.

1650 Highway 351

by Brandon Peña

The Wal-Mart Supercenter on the north side of Abilene opened its doors in 2005. It joined a second Wal-Mart Supercenter location in southwest Abilene. The addition of this store heralded a major trend at the beginning of the twenty-first century—movement of the commercial centers to the far northeastern and southeastern parts of the city, anchored by what have become symbols of American mass consumer retailing and the increasing homogenization of the marketplace. The construction of this second Wal-Mart Supercenter was part of a strategy by local developers to meet a perceived demand for additional inexpensive retail shopping in the northern section of the city, while creating an economic stimulus that would increase property values on that side of town. With it would come the development of new neighborhoods and subdivisions, sports and leisure complexes, and other facilities on land that, unlike other parts of town, remain wide open and largely unbounded by existing or historical development, and convenient to major transportation arteries.

With the opening of Abilene's second Wal-Mart Supercenter, the area around the intersection of Highway 351 and I-20 blossomed with the addition of new national-chain restaurants, national chain home-improvement stores, and national chain hotels. Wal-Mart is currently the world's largest public corporation by revenue, providing goods ranging from clothes to food. Historically, several allied and affiliated retailers follow in the wake of Wal-Mart in a lucrative market forumla proven sucessful across the country. These stores occupy strip shopping centers nearby, creating a large retail complex that appeals to consumers interested in predictable and affordable pricing reflecting national tastes over regional influences.

Ambler Avenue and Judge Ely Boulevard

by Terran Ragland

Abilene Christian University has one of the best baseball playing fields in the country, but this was not always the case. After decades without one, the university decided to bring back its baseball program in February of 1990. The administration wanted to provide the program with a top-notch facility. This was the birth of Crutcher Scott Field. Abilene Christian alumnus Crutcher Scott, an Abilene oilman who also served on the city council, is the namesake of the field. Scott and his family were the major supporters for the project. Another noteworthy contributor was major league great Nolan Ryan. Ryan played in the pros with former player and head coach Bill Gilbreth and allowed ACU to use his name for two benefit dinners to raise funds for the field totaling more than $150,000. The massive complex seats 4,000 and is equipped with major-league caliber lighting.

The first game played at the new field took place on February 23, 1991 with an Abilene Christian 2-1 win over Tarleton State University. Crutcher Scott Field has played host to many high school playoff games, college tournaments, and the NCAA Division II South Central regional tournament. Also, Crutcher Scott Field was the home stadium for the Abilene Prairie Dogs, a minor league team in the now-defunct Texas-Louisiana League, from 1995 to 1999.

2200 Hickory Street

by Gail Adlesperger

The Logsdon Chapel was constructed in 1988 as part of the new Logsdon School of Theology at Hardin-Simmons University. Thanks to a generous gift by Mr. and Mrs. Charles Logsdon of Abilene, the chapel now sits at the southeast corner of the university with its enormous stained glass widow facing the corner like a peaceful beacon of Christian art, welcoming anyone who should pass by.

Logsdon Chapel, with a 350-seat capacity, has a variety of uses to the campus and the community. A few of the special uses of the chapel are for the Logsdon Seminary chapel services, state and regional conferences for pastors and churches, guest speakers on the Hardin-Simmons campus, various community events, university concerts, organ recitals, and weddings.

Two of the chapel's prominent features are the stained glass window at its front and the Vissar-Rowland Opus 93 pipe organ at its back. The thirty-by-forty-foot stained glass window was a gift from Mrs. Charles Logsdon. It was designed as

a single element but constructed in sixty individual panels on metal framework. Three important elements of the window signify the purpose, mission, and vision of Logsdon School of Theology: a cross in the center, pointing to the centrality of Christ in each believer and student; the open bible represents the commitment to educate and guide by the authority of scripture; and the dove represents the Holy Spirit and the global mission of the church. All are placed upon a field of color and concentric circles representing the world in which each student is called to serve.

Officially named the Grace Katherine White Organ, a gift from Mrs. Katherine Logsdon White, the organ was constructed in 1992 from Appalachian Red Oak with keys made of ebony and maple in the traditional North German-Dutch design with a distinctively French character. Occupying the majority of the chapel's balcony this organ is the visually stunning balance to the stained glass window. This chapel is a true landmark for all who pass.

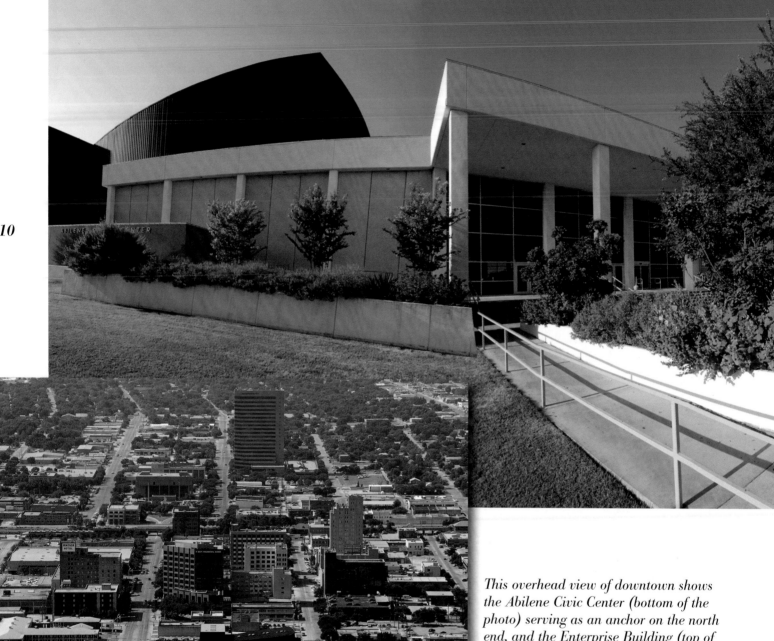

This overhead view of downtown shows the Abilene Civic Center (bottom of the photo) serving as an anchor on the north end, and the Enterprise Building (top of the photo) looming to the south. The eclectic collection of architectural styles in this photo reveals a great deal about how the town developed over the years. Notice the railroad tracks bisecting the town.

1100 North Sixth Street

by Kristina Green

By the 1960s, Abilene citizens wanted to add amenities to their city that reflected its growing sophistication and maturity. They approved bonds for the construction of the Abilene Civic Center at 1100 North Sixth Street in 1967. Completed in November 1970, the auditorium of the building has more than 2,100 seats, including a 700-seat balcony. It also has a 72-foot by 70-foot stage, complete with a hydraulically operated orchestra pit. Over the decades, the stage has seen performances from world-famous singers and the casts of Broadway musicals.

The Civic Center also features a conference center with more than 13,000 square feet. In addition, it holds a 20,000-square-foot exhibit hall. The outside of the building includes a nicely landscaped plaza with fountain, trees, and year-round plantings.

Today, the Abilene Civic Center hosts more than 700 events annually and generates more than $3 million in convention spending and nearly four times that in collateral and associated spending by out of town attendees in places like local hotels, restaurants, attractions, and gas stations. Additionally, the Civic Center supports active little-theater groups, ballet companies, a civic chorus, an art museum, the Abilene Philharmonic Orchestra, and an opera association. For more than forty years, the Abilene Civic Center has fulfilled its mission to the people of Abilene.

211

This aerial view of the Abilene Civic Center from the northwest shows the various components of the complex, including auditorium at the top of the photo, and meeting halls attached.

1420 North Third Street

by Ben Newland

In 1885, four years after Abilene's founding, some residents came together to form the First Christian Church, holding services in the schoolhouse located on the corner of North Third and Cedar Streets. Somewhere around 1900, the church body put a thousand dollar down payment on property at North Third and Hickory, funded by the Ladies Aid Society. In 1902, the First Christian Church organized the construction of a large auditorium on the land. The church held services at this auditorium until 1921, when the building burned to the ground after the explosion of a gas stove that had been lit to warm the building for a baptism. Later that year, the church funded the construction of a new building. In 1970 the congregation built the current structure, demolishing the 1921 building once they had finished construction on the new one.

The current building is an elegant mixture of elements from multiple different architectural styles. The façade is transposed from the front area of the Parthenon, even down to the color scheme and column arrangement. This reworking of classical elements, suggests an almost neoclassical flavor to the design. On the other hand, this structure, including the steeple, is a good example of New England colonial meetinghouse architecture.

213

214

FRONTI

This aerial view from the north showcases the interesting architecture of Frontier Texas! and its use of elements inspired by the various forts in the region to create a landmark facility on the east side of downtown. Notice the school buses in the circular drive, the faux chimneys, and the buffalo sculpture to the right. The pickup owned by one of the authors is in the parking lot.

625 North First Street

by Gail Adlesperger

If you want to step back in time, then Frontier Texas!, a 14,000-square-foot building situated on 6.4 acres of land in downtown Abilene, designed to welcome, entertain, and educate is the place to go. It is a welcoming gateway into the Downtown area when coming in from the east on Business Interstate 20 and also the trailhead for the 700 miles of the Forts Trail Loop that starts and stops in Abilene. Frontier Texas covers the history of this region from 1780 to 1880, as it was a time of great change just prior to the railroad development in West Texas, the prologue to the founding of Abilene.

In 1999 the Texas Department of Transportation announced the T-21 Reimbursement Program, and volunteers began planning a visitor center that would also productively use a scruffy industrial site as part of their Downtown Revitalization Program. They chose a newly acquired seven-acre lot that had been used for decades as a railroad storage yard and a commercial recycling center.

The architecture of Frontier Texas furthers the objectives to welcome, entertain, and educate. With it being the start and stop of the Forts Trail loop it needed to have a resemblance to the Forts of the time giving an inspiration for the major design of the facility. In the front of Frontier Texas are four enormous stone chimneys mimicking the structures that remain today of Fort Phantom Hill, a few miles to the north of Abilene. To recognize another major economic draw of the region more than a century ago, the site also boasts a nine-foot, hollow-cast bronze buffalo, situated on a cement etched drawing of Texas surrounded by prairie grass in front of the chimneys. He symbolically gazes southward toward Buffalo Gap.

The facility is a visitor center and a high tech, interactive trip into the past. Within the interactive center there is a Welcome Theater that introduces some of the people that shaped this region and a little information on the history of the region, items of the time displayed such as pelts, guns, Indian utensils, a Stage Coach, a wagon, and an Orientation Theater. In the parade field on the sides and rear of Frontier Texas are Military Formation Stones arranged like a military formation would have lined up on a parade field. The parade field is used at various times of the year for heritage days, summer camps, social gatherings, and re-enactments.

2549 South First Street

by Kerri Bristow

The first ever Taco Bueno restaurant was founded by Bill Waugh in 1967 in the building at 2549 South First. As the restaurant chain expanded, major food distributors bought it out, turning the brand into an important regional franchise. Today, Taco Bueno has more than 160 stores and is present in eleven states. Abilene currently has four Taco Bueno locations—but not in the original building. This structure has been used for a variety of businesses over the years, including other restaurants and a daycare facility.

217

500 Chestnut Street

by Gail Adlesperger

This high-rise building is one of the first buildings you see as you approach Abilene. Constructed in 1984 with twenty floors of office space, it is the tallest building in Abilene at 283 feet. The Enterprise Building design is a combination of classical and uncommon, with its notched corner bays and a brick exterior highlighted by an array of windows. One of the major highlights is the first five stories of the building that create a dramatic atrium on the north end of the building.

The Enterprise Building is owned and used by Musgrave Enterprises, and the additional office spaces are leased to various other companies. The Bank of America leases the whole lobby floor of the building adding their name to the top outside of the building, resulting in people also sometimes referring to the building as the Bank of America Building. The Enterprise Building also has a basement floor that houses a food court, beauty shop, and shoe shining station.

There is nothing usual about the interior design of the Enterprise Building. Starting with its floors of 62,000 square feet of Chassagne marble quarried and imported from Rocamat, France, and then cut and fabricated in Carthage, Missouri, to its magnificent carpeting and hardwood flooring. It has wide corridors with nine-foot slab doors, accessible only with computer security cards and a state-of-the-art security system with constant video monitoring. The Enterprise Building also houses a main vault made of 1,650,000 pounds of concrete and 77,000 pounds of reinforcing steel. Although the Enterprise Building was built a century after the founding of Abilene, it stands tall with a sense of permanence as the city moves into the future.

300 Oak Street

by Malaney Lopez

Since the organization of Taylor County, it has had four courthouses. The current Taylor County Courthouse is located at 300 Oak Street. It was built in 1972 and designed by Architects Tittle, Luther, Loving, and Lee. The exterior is made of concrete and pink granite. The current courthouse is modern style, and the exterior has little unnecessary detail and is a simple in form. This "international" style first appeared in the post World War II era and became very popular as an architectural break with old conventions that spoke of new and progressive trend that mirrored the times. As in other contemporary styles of architecture, the Taylor County Courthouse can be considered bold with its extremely simple and functional design.

2070 Zoo Lane, Nelson Park

by Jennifer Wells

The Abilene Zoo got its start in what is now known as Rose Park. Among the animals kept at the first zoo, most notable were lions, whose roar from their cages in the cinderblock building could be heard for miles around. In 1966, however, the Abilene Zoological Gardens moved to its current location off of Highway 36 at Nelson Park.

The zoo is home to around 173 species of animals. Abilene's Zoo includes a Wetlands Boardwalk, Creepy Crawlers Center, and animals exhibits such as black rhinos, jaguars, lions, bears, giraffes, reptiles, and more. One unique experience the Abilene Zoo offers is a chance to feed all the animals except the monkeys. The giraffe enclosure even has a bridge where visitors can stand at eye-level with the graceful creatures and feed crackers to them by placing the tasty morsel on the giraffe's tongue. The Abilene Zoological Gardens represent a significant landmark in the city, showcasing some of the best attractions residents and visitors alike, and is the only Texas zoo of note west of Fort Worth and east of El Paso.

224

This view of the Taylor County Expo Center complex, looking northwest, illustrates a number of interesting features about Abilene. Downtown shows up distinctly to the upper right, with several landmarks mentioned in the book clearly visible. The Enterprise Building also makes a bold statement to the left. The proximity of Shotwell Stadium to the Expo Center is also apparent. Notice, too, the large number of horse trailers around the various barns and arenas of the facility, revealing its popularity as a rodeo, cutting horse, livestock show, and roping venue.

1700 Highway 36

by Derek Peterson

225

One of Abilene's most popular attractions is the Taylor County Exposition Center (commonly called the Expo Center). It is a great source of revenue for Taylor County as well as the City of Abilene, considering the amount of tourism it attracts to the area. The compound is approximately 117 acres and is comprised of the Coliseum, Outdoor Arena, Entertainment Pavilion, Horse Barn, Big Country Hall, Round Building, Display Building, Modern Living Hall, and Livestock Barn.

The area along State Highway 36 first boasted show barns and a rodeo arena in the late 1950s. Then in 1961, the citizens of Taylor County failed to pass a $1.5 million bond election to build a coliseum. Six years later, however, voters approved a $1.75 million bond issue to build the coliseum and make improvements to the fairgrounds. The new Taylor County Coliseum was completed in 1969. With all of the variety of venues at the Expo Center, this facility hosts multiple events throughout the year, including the county fair, the circus, rodeos, and the famous Western Heritage Classic. In addition, events ranging from monster truck shows, professional wrestling events, and concerts all occur at different times at this venue. The Coliseum once served as the home for the now defunct Abilene Aviators Hockey Team. Events at the Expo Center are posted throughout the year.

717 East Industrial Boulevard

by Jennifer Wells and Michael Jerry Akin

Cisco Junior College got its start in 1909 as the Britton Training Institute, a private school in Cisco, Texas, named for its founder O.C. Britton. Unfortunately, World War I caused such a drastic drop in students that the school closed. From 1923 to 1932, the Christian Church of Texas tried to revive the old college as a four-year, church based school called Randolph College. The college, however, suffered monetary problems and struggled to operate as a two-year school from 1932 to 1936, but to no avail as the doors closed once again. Cisco Junior College reopened in 1939 as a component of the Cisco Independent School District. In 1956, Cisco Junior College successfully separated from the public school system, energized by a flood of government spending and the post war G.I. Bill.

Cisco first placed a branch in Abilene in the late 1990s, but in 2004, the college built a $7.5 million, 72,000-square-foot campus off of Industrial Boulevard at Loop 322. The Abilene Education Center includes 38 classrooms, 16 labs, and a new library.

Another advantage this new campus has is that the industrial trades that were taught away from the main campus before are now taught at the main campus. There are an additional four classrooms and four labs just for the vocational trade instruction. In the time since its construction, the campus has already served as an anchor for other businesses to build along the loop, making it one of the fastest-growing areas of the city in the beginning of the twenty-first century.

6250 Highway 83/84 at Antilley Road

by Anders Jordan Leverton

In 1968 a group physicians and other investors pooled their resources to create the West Texas Medical Center in Abilene, timed to benefit from new government spending through the Medicaid and Medicare programs while also caring for the needs of an aging population that had, previously, only had limited access to healthcare. Just two years later, in 1970, the cardiology team of this new hospital performed the first heart catheterization and open-heart surgery in the Midwest Texas area. As the next decade passed, the hospital had trouble accommodating new technological advances in its original building. In 1984, the hospital sold to the Humana Healthcare Corporation which built new facilities at its current address. Another advantage of this new property was that it would allow room for expansion. Over the years the facility has been owned by several national healthcare corporations, including the current owners Triad Hospitals of Plano, Texas, and Community Health Systems of Franklin, Tennessee. In 1991, the hospital changed its name once again—taking on the now-familiar "Abilene Regional Medical Center."

Abilene Regional's purpose is to enhance the quality of patients' lives, and provide innovative patient centered healthcare. These goals are illustrated by the fact that Regional's success rate for open-heart surgery not only surpasses the state average, it exceeds the national average as well. Also, demonstrating their commitment to their patients, Regional is always updating, giving their patients the best care possible. In 1992, Regional added the Heart & Vascular Institute to the building. In 2004, the hospital added the new Women's Center.

Today, Abilene Regional Medical Center is a sprawling complex with more than two hundred physicians and another seven hundred employees. It has 231 beds, and is centered in one of the fastest growing areas of the city. It has quickly become an anchoring landmark to the southern entrance to Abilene.

2617 Antilley Road

by Jennifer Wells

Demonstrating the continued growth of the south side of Abilene, the Wesley Court Retirement Center opened its doors at 2617 Antilley Road in the fall of 2004 to service the needs of an aging Abilene population. The glass-fronted two-story lobby faces the road, with luxurious chandeliers and well-appointed interior design evident to passersby. Behind the large entrance, however, the property spans fifty acres. The center is part of the Sears Methodist Retirement System and provides state-of-the-art facilities to the residents, who can choose from a wide variety of living facilities including 30 Executive Homes, 81 Apartments, 19 Assisted Living Units, and 30 Health Care Center Beds. There are also a number of recreational accommodations available, including an onsite wellness center, library, barber/beauty shop, and walking trails. The site also features an expansive lake covering a portion of the property. With the addition of this facility, the south end of the city is clearly an area that will see continued development in the years to come, spurred on by investments and developments in healthcare.

231

3430 Antilley Road

by Kristina Green

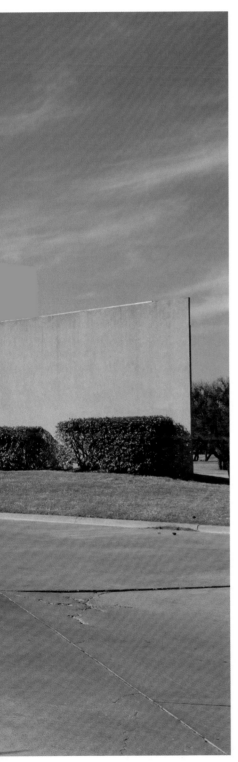

The story of Abilene's growth to the south and its historic ties to the petroleum industry come together in the Wylie United Methodist Church building at 3430 Antilley Road. In the second half of the twentieth century, the LaJet Corporation became a major competitor in the oil refinement business. During the oil boom years of the 1970s, the company built its headquarters building on Antilley road, next to the brand new Fairway Oaks Golf and Racquet Club, which opened April 5, 1979 with several LaJet principals as its developers. This oil-fueled economy brought significant wealth and construction to the south side of Abilene.

Beginning in 1981, the LaJet Corporation sponsored a golf tournament at Fairway Oaks that was added to the PGA Tour—the LaJet Classic. By the mid-1980s, however, the oil market was no longer stable, and in 1987, LaJet Corporation went out of business. The LaJet property on Antilley stayed virtually unused for five years. Wylie United Methodist Church, which had been founded in 1902, had outgrown the capacity of its old sanctuary on Buffalo Gap Road, and in 1992, they purchased the building. After extensive renovation, the congregation moved in, and still today, windows of the church look out onto the 11th hole of the Fairway Oaks Golf Course—the same view the LaJet executives used to have.

233

4310 Buffalo Gap Road

by Anders Jordan Leverton

The Mall of Abilene was in March 1979, with the purpose of providing consumers a safe and comfortable place to shop. The anchor department stores at the opening of the new center were Sears, J.C. Penney's, Dillard's, and a long-time Abilene name, Grisham's; of those four, Grisham's is the only one not there today.

Since 1979, the mall has grown with the arrival of new retail businesses, as it is has averaged 90% occupancy. Aside from new store designs, the Mall as a whole has had only one renovation on the building, which was in 2005. Under this transformation, the management revamped the interior with new tiles and carpeting and removed fountains. The exterior of the building remained relatively unchanged, with the exception of adding new signs to the entrances.

Perhaps one of the most important features making the Mall of Abilene a landmark, is its effect on the economy of Abilene. It is the largest taxpayer in the area, which funds a significant amount of local public education. It also strengthens the economy by providing jobs and bringing in retail stores that appeal to the public.

A bird's eye view of the area around the Mall of Abilene demonstrates the powerful impact it has had on the development of Abilene's south side. Notice the wide variety of national chain restaurants and retailers around the periphery, the presence of a bank at the top of the photo, and the hotels to the right. U.S. Highway 83/84 to the bottom left is undergoing expansion to handle the increase in traffic.

REFERENCES

#1 Knight-Sayles Cabin
Frazier, Donald S., Robert F. Pace, Robert P. Wettemann, Jr. *The Texas You Expect: The Story of Buffalo Gap Historic Village.* Abilene: State House Press, 2006.
Zachry, Juanita Daniel. *Buffalo Gap Historic Village.* Austin: Nortex Press, 1992.

#2 Boone-Riddell House
Frazier, Donald S., Robert F. Pace, Robert P. Wettemann, Jr. *The Texas You Expect: The Story of Buffalo Gap Historic Village.* Abilene: State House Press, 2006.

#3 Marshal Tom Hill House
Frazier, Donald S., Robert F. Pace, Robert P. Wettemann, Jr. *The Texas You Expect: The Story of Buffalo Gap Historic Village.* Abilene: State House Press, 2006.
Zachry, Juanita Daniel. *Buffalo Gap Historic Village.* Austin: Nortex Press, 1992.

#4 Original Taylor County Courthouse and Jail
Frazier, Donald S., Robert F. Pace, Robert P. Wettemann, Jr. *The Texas You Expect: The Story of Buffalo Gap Historic Village.* Abilene: State House Press, 2006.
Zachry, Juanita Daniel. *Buffalo Gap Historic Village.* Austin: Nortex Press, 1992.

#5 The Old Taylor County Courthouse
Taylor County Courthouse of 1915: Historic Courthouse Master Plan. Abilene: Tippett & Gee, Ltd, 2001.

#6 The Superintendent's House, Abilene State School
"Abilene State School 1899 to Present: A Century of Service." Pamphlet. Abilene: Abilene State School, 1999.
City of Abilene. *Abilene Historic Landmarks.* Abilene, TX: City of Abilene. 1987; updated, 1990.

#7 Old Administration Building, Abilene State School
"Abilene State School 1899 to Present: A Century of Service." Pamphlet. Abilene: Abilene State School, 1999.
City of Abilene. *Abilene Historic Landmarks.* Abilene, TX: City of Abilene. 1987; updated, 1990.
Feemster, David, Abilene State School Historian, Interview with Kensey Allen, October 24, 2004, Abilene, TX.
Whitaker, Bill. "Body & Mind & School's Off-Beat Past Grounded in Hope." *Abilene Reporter News.* September 19, 1999.

#8 Cockrell House
City of Abilene. *Abilene Historic Landmarks.* Abilene, TX: City of Abilene. 1987; updated, 1990.
Duff, Katharyn, with Betty Kay Seibt. *Catclaw Country.* Burnet, Texas: Eakin Press, 1980.
Hasink, Pamela. "Lytle Lake." The Handbook of Texas Online. http://www.tsha.utexas.edu/handbook/online/articles/view/LL/rol98.html. Accessed November 4, 2004.

#9 Ham House
City of Abilene. *Abilene Historic Landmarks.* Abilene, TX: City of Abilene. 1987; updated, 1990.
Ham, Beth. Interview with Leah Herod. October 20, 2004, Abilene, Texas.
"Zack T. Adams." Available at the Historic Preservation Planning Office, City Hall, Abilene, Texas.

#10 Kirby House
City of Abilene. *Abilene Historic Landmarks.* Abilene, TX: City of Abilene. 1987; updated, 1990.
Craven. Jackie. "Architecture." About.com. http://architecture.about.com/cs/housestyles/a/queenanne.htm. Accessed November 1, 2004.
North, Jack. *Pioneers of the Abilene Area, Vol. 1.* Abilene: Quality Printing Co., 1978.

#11 Watson-Hopkin House
City of Abilene. *Abilene Historic Landmarks.* Abilene, TX: City of Abilene. 1987; updated, 1990.
_____. "Research Data Sheet." Abilene, TX: City of Abilene. 1988-89.

#12 Sayles/Jones/Stevens/Bowen House
City of Abilene. *Abilene Historic Landmarks.* Abilene, TX: City of Abilene. 1987; updated, 1990.
Architecture in Abilene. Abilene: Abilene Preservation League, 2000.

#13 Sayles-Dillard House
Dillard, Richard. "National Register of Historic Places Inventory – Nomination Form: Henry Sayles Home, Abilene Texas." January 8, 1976. Sayles File, Abilene Preservation League, Abilene, Texas.
"Sayles Boulevard Historic District." Typewritten report. Sayles File, Abilene Preservation League, Abilene, Texas.
Sayles, E.B. (Ted) to Seth Sayles. May 2, 1977. Sayles File, Abilene Preservation League, Abilene, Texas.

#14 Dodd-Harkrider House
Historic Resources Survey of Abilene, completed by Donald and Lora Christensen. Abilene Preservation League, Abilene, Texas.

#15 Evans-McCloskey House
Blaschke, Carrie. Interview with Catherine Watjen. December 1, 2004. Abilene, Texas.
City of Abilene. *Abilene Historic Landmarks.* Abilene, TX: City of Abilene. 1987; updated, 1990.
Craven, Jackie. "Architecture." About.com. http://architecture.about.com/cs/housestyles/a/queenanne.htm. Accessed November 1, 2004;

#16 Ackerman-Chapman House
City of Abilene. *Abilene Historic Landmarks.* Abilene, TX: City of Abilene. 1987; updated, 1990.

#17 Motz House
City of Abilene. *Abilene Historic Landmarks.* Abilene, TX: City of Abilene. 1987; updated, 1990.
"Gambrel." Archiseek Website. http://www.archiseek.com/guides/glossary/t.html. Accessed October 10, 2004.
"House Styles: Colonial-Revival." About.com Website. http://architecture.about.com/library/bl-colonialrevival.htm. Accessed October 10, 2004.

#18 Swenson House
City of Abilene. *Abilene Historic Landmarks.* Abilene, TX: City of Abilene. 1987; updated, 1990.
Duff, Katharyn. "Drama, Courage Fill Business History." *Abilene Reporter-News.* December 5, 1965.
"Swenson House." Typewritten report. Swenson File, Abilene Preservation League, Abilene, Texas.

#19 Cowden-Godbout House
"1802 Swenson," Typewritten Report. Abilene Preservation League, Abilene, Texas.
"The Houses that Sears Built: Everything You Ever Wanted to Know About Mail-order Homes, 2002." Gentle Beam Publication. http://www.old-
    houseweb.com/stories/Detailed/10426.shtml. Accessed October 12, 2004.

#20 Marston Gym, Hardin-Simmons University
"History of the Polk-Key City Basketball Tournament." Hardin-Simmons University Website.
    http://www.hsutx.edu/academics/irvin_edu/fssc/pkc/history/. Accessed February 21, 2008.
Morrow, Merlin. Interview with Terann Ragland. February 18, 2008. Abilene, Texas.

#21 Old Cotton Warehouse
Ellis, L. Tuffly. "Cotton Compress Industry." Handbook of Texas Online. http://www.tshaonline.org/handbook/online/articles/CC/drc2.html.
    Accessed February 26, 2008.

#22 Pfeifer Building
"Downtown Walking Tour." Abilene Visitors and Convention Bureau Website. http://www.abilenevisitors.com/visitors/historicwalkingtour4.html.
    Accessed February 22, 2008.
"Walter Pfeifer Jr. Obituary." *Abilene Reporter-News.* http://www.zoominfo.com/Search/PersonDetail.aspx?PersonID=528774974. Accessed Feb-
    ruary 22, 2008.

#23 T&P Freight Warehouse
"Historic Preservation Certification Application." T&P File, Abilene Preservation League, Abilene, Texas.
Percival, Pamela. "City Gets T&P Depot." *Abilene Reporter News.* February 15, 1991.
Tozar, Lindsay. "T&P Warehouse Close to Becoming The Railhead Grill" *Abilene Reporter News.* October 7, 1998.
Williamson, Doug. "Railhead Will Close: City Spent $2 Million on Building" *Abilene Reporter News.* November 15, 2000.

#24 The Grace Museum
"Grace Museum File." Abilene Preservation League, Abilene, Texas.
The Grace Museum Website. http://www.thegracemuseum.org/about_grace/about.html. Accessed October 12, 2004.

#25 Cypress Building
City of Abilene. *Abilene Historic Landmarks.* Abilene, TX: City of Abilene. 1987; updated, 1990.
Zachry, Juanita Daniel. *A Living History: Taylor Country and the Big Country.* Abilene: Quality Press, 1999.

#26 The Elks Building
"Elks Art Center." Abilene Preservation League Website. http://www.abilenepreservation.org/elks/index.htm. Accessed February 21, 2008.

#27 T&P Depot
Butman, Wilma. Interview with Anders Jordan Leverton. February 17, 2008. Abilene, Texas.
City of Abilene. *Abilene Historic Landmarks.* Abilene, TX: City of Abilene. 1987; updated, 1990.

#28 The Old Weather Bureau Building
City of Abilene. *Abilene Historic Landmarks.* Abilene, TX: City of Abilene. 1987; updated, 1990.
Fulton, Loretta. "Cottonseed, Part of Rose's Life." Abilene Biz Website. October 26, 2007. http://www.reporternews.com/news/2007/Oct/26/
    cottonseed-part-roses-life/. Accessed February 22, 2008.

#29 Pegues-Jennings House (Hickory Street Café)
Dromgoole, Glenn. "Hickory Street Café Known for its Chicken Salad, Zucchini Bread." *Abilene Reporter-News*. October 13, 2000.

#30 Old Main, McMurry University
City of Abilene. *Abilene Historic Landmarks*. Abilene, TX: City of Abilene. 1987; updated, 1990.
Cosby, Hugh E. et al. *History of Abilene*. Abilene: Cosby, 1955.
Downs, Fane, and Robert W. Sledge. *Pride of our Western Prairies*. Abilene: McMurry College, 1989.

#31 Duffy-Wright House
"Abilene Register of Historic Properties." National Register of Historic Places.
    http://www.abilenetx.com/planningservices/documents/AbileneRegisterofHistoricProperties_000.pdf. Accessed February 22, 2008.

#32 Campbell-McDonald House
"Abilene Register of Historic Properties." National Register of Historic Places.
    http://www.abilenetx.com/planningservices/documents/AbileneRegisterofHistoricProperties_000.pdf. Accessed February 22, 2008.

#33 Fulwiler-Schoultz House
"Abilene Founder Lion's Club History." Abilene Founder Lion's Club Hompepage. http://www.geocities.com/Pentagon/Bunker/4819/.
    Accessed February 22, 2008.
"Abilene Register of Historic Properties." National Register of Historic Places.
    http://www.abilenetx.com/planningservices/documents/AbileneRegisterofHistoricProperties_000.pdf. Accessed February 22, 2008.

#34 Nichol-Jennings House
"Sayles Boulevard Historic District." Abilene Preservation League, Abilene, Texas.
Walker, Lester. *American Shelter*. Woodstock, NY: The Overlook Press, 1997.

#35 Highland Church of Christ
"A Brief History of the Highland Church of Christ." Highland Church of Christ Website.
    http://www.highlandchurch.org/about/history. Accessed February 23, 2008.

#36 Alta Vista Elementary School
"Alta Vista Elementary School Information," SchoolTree.Org. http://schooltree.org/480744000011.html. Accessed November 10, 2004.
DeJesus, Thaddeus. "Schools Cope with Closing Plan." *Abilene Reporter-News*. February 1, 2003.
Levesque, Sidney. "AISD to Find Uses for Closed Schools." *Abilene Reporter-News*. July 13, 2003.
Schuhmann, Sidney. "Against the Odds: Elementaries Excel by Pushing Reading Skills," Abilene Reporter-News Online.
    http://texnews.com/1998/2002/local/read0528.html. Accessed November 9, 2004.

#37 Kaufman-Hanna House
Middleton, Jaynne. Interview with Crissi Renaye Reneau. October 15, 2004. Abilene, Texas.

#38 Lincoln Middle School
City of Abilene. *Abilene Historic Landmarks*. Abilene, TX: City of Abilene. 1987; updated, 1990.
Coates, Shelby. "AISD Bond Package." Big Country Home Page. http://bigcountryhomepage.com/content/fulltext/?cid=5738.
    Accessed February 21, 2008.
Humphrey, Joe. Interview with Trey Cox. November 14, 2004. Abilene, Texas.
McPeak, Donovan. "Let's Salvage Lincoln, But Not as a School." *Abilene Reporter-News*. April 2003.

#39 Old Fire Station #2
City of Abilene. *Abilene Historic Landmarks*. Abilene, TX: City of Abilene. 1987; updated, 1990.
Lewis, Jeff. Interview with Trey Cox. November 12, 2004. Abilene, Texas.
Test, Sandy. "FIRE! At the Cry, Volunteers Came Running as Pros Now Do." *Abilene Reporter-News*. April 1981.
Whitaker, Bill. "Attorneys Fired Up About New Office." *Abilene Reporter-News*. October 1992.

#40 George W. and Lavina McDaniel House
City of Abilene. *Abilene Historic Landmarks*. Abilene, TX: City of Abilene. 1987; updated, 1990.

#41 Park Office Building
Abel, Nancy. "Lauren Construction." Flyer. Available at Lauren Construction, Abilene, Texas.
City of Abilene. *Abilene Historic Landmarks*. Abilene, TX: City of Abilene. 1987; updated, 1990.
"Renaissance Revival." City of Chicago Website. http://www.ci.chi.il.us/landmarks/stylebuide/renaissancerevival.html. Accessed November 1, 2004.
Tate, Curtis. "Abilene's Golden Era: The Emergence of a West Texas City During the 1920s." Unpublished Masters Thesis, Hardin Simmons
    University, 1991.

#42 Burlington Railroad Depot
"Burlington Route, A Brief Texas History." http://home.austin.rr.com/aldossantos/burlington_route.htm. Accessed February 23, 2008.
City of Abilene. *Abilene Historic Landmarks*. Abilene, TX: City of Abilene. 1987; updated, 1990.
Keike, Carl. "Col. Morgan Jones Helped Bring Railroad to Abilene." *Abilene Reporter-News*. January 27, 2006.

#43 West Texas Utilities Power & Ice Plant
City of Abilene. *Abilene Historic Landmarks*. Abilene, TX: City of Abilene. 1987; updated, 1990.
"WTU Timeline." Abilene Reporter-News Archives Online. http://www.texnews.com/local97/wtu2122397.html. Accessed February 23, 2008.

#44 Gulf Distribution Building
"Gulf Oil Corporation." *Handbook of Texas Online*. http://www.tsha.utexas.edu/handbook/online/articles/view/GG/dog2.html.
    Accessed November 14, 2004
Worley, John F. *Abilene City Directory 1926*. Dallas, Tex,: John F. Worley Directory Co., Compilers and Publishers, 1926.
_____. *Abilene City Directory 1931*. Dallas, Tex,: John F. Worley Directory Co., Publishers, 1931.
_____. *Abilene (Taylor County) City Directory 1936*. Dallas, Tex.: John F. Worley Directory Co., Publishers, 1936.
_____. *Abilene (Taylor County) City Directory 1953*. Dallas, Tex.: John F. Worley Directory Co., Publishers, 1953.

#45 Hilton (Windsor) Hotel
Beal, Sandy. "The Windsor Hotel." Brochure available at the Windsor Apartments.
City of Abilene. *Abilene Historic Landmarks*. Abilene, TX: City of Abilene. 1987; updated, 1990.
DeJesus, Thaddeus. "Architect on Wooten Project is Familiar with Historic Restoration." *Abilene Reporter News*. August 8, 2004.
Duff, Katharyn, with Betty Kay Seibt. *Catclaw Country*. Burnet, Texas: Eakin Press, 1980.
Morrison, Michael E. "The Windsor-Rebirth of Abilene's Downtown: Project Summary." Abilene, TX: Department of Economic Development, 1995.

#46 The Minter Building
City of Abilene. *Abilene Historic Landmarks*. Abilene, TX: City of Abilene. 1987; updated, 1990.
_____. "Research Data Sheet." Abilene, TX: City of Abilene. 1988-89.
U.S. Department of the Interior. "National Register of Historic Places Continuation Sheet." Washington: National Park Service, 1982.

#47 Alexander Building
"Abilene Commercial Historic District." Typed Report. Alexander File. Abilene Preservation League, Abilene, Texas
"Alexander Building Plan Announced" *Abilene Reporter News*. March 2, 1999.
City of Abilene. *Abilene Historic Landmarks*. Abilene, TX: City of Abilene. 1987; updated, 1990.
Architectural Styles of America On-line Inquiry. http://jan.ucc.nau.edu/~twp/architecture/neoclassiacl. Accessed November 14, 2004.

#48 Compton Building (Cypress Street Station)
City of Abilene. *Abilene Historic Landmarks*. Abilene, TX: City of Abilene. 1987; updated, 1990.
Meiron, Pat. "Downtown Revival: Where Old Mingles Gracefully with New." Abilene Reporter News: Inside-Abilene. http://www.inside-abilene.com/
    downtown/downtown.html. Accessed November 15, 2004.
Shew, Brenda. Interview with Sara Ritson. November 16, 2004. Abilene, Texas.

#49 Johnson and Gorsuch Building
City of Abilene. *Abilene Historic Landmarks*. Abilene, TX: City of Abilene. 1987; updated, 1990.
Tate, Curtis. "Abilene's Golden Era: The Emergence of a West Texas City During the 1920s." Unpublished Masters Thesis, Hardin Simmons
    University, 1991.

#50 Rhodes Automotive Building (NCCIL)
NCCIL Website, http://www.nccil.org. Accessed October 9, 2004.
"Rhodes Automotive" File. Abilene Preservation League. Abilene, Texas.

#51 Caldwell House
"Many Traditions Begun at 790 Orange." *Abilene Reporter News*. October 12, 1978.
"Parramore Addition." Typewritten report. Parramore District File, Abilene Preservation League, Abilene, Texas.

#52 First Central Presbyterian Church
"History of the Church." First Central Presbyterian Church Website. http://www.fcpc.net/history.asp. Accessed February 19, 2008.

#53 Minter House
Abilene Register of Historic Properties. City of Abilene Website. http://www.abilenetx.com/historic/historic_register.htm.
    Accessed November 15, 2004.
City of Abilene. *Abilene Historic Landmarks*. Abilene, TX: City of Abilene. 1987; updated, 1990.
Duff, Katharyn, with Betty Kay Seibt. *Catclaw Country*. Burnet, Texas: Eakin Press, 1980.
Moore, David. "National Register of Historic Places Registration Form." January 1992. Available at the Abilene Preservation League, Abilene, Texas.

#54 Stith House
City of Abilene. *Abilene Historic Landmarks.* Abilene, TX: City of Abilene. 1987; updated, 1990.
"House Styles: Tudor-Revival." About.com. http://architecture.about.com/library/bl-tudorrevival.htm. Accessed October 10, 2004.
"Will Stith." *Genealogy Magazine.* http://www.genealogymagazine.com/willstith.html. Accessed October 9, 2004.

#55 George R. Davis House
Architecture in Abilene. Abilene: Abilene Preservation League, 2000.
Historic Preservation Comprehensive Plan: City of Abilene. Texas. Abilene: Planned and Community Development Department, 1977.
"Texas-Taylor County." National Register of Historic Places Website. http://www.nationalhistoricalregister.com/TX/Taylor/state.html.
    Accessed October 20, 2004.

#56 Abilene Streetcar Barn
City of Abilene. *Abilene Historic Landmarks.* Abilene, TX: City of Abilene. 1987; updated, 1990.
Zachry, Juanita Daniel. *Abilene: The Key City.* Northridge California; Windsor Publishing, Inc. 1986.

#57 Higginbotham House
"2102 Swenson File." Abilene Preservation League, Abilene, Texas.
"RIBA." Architecture.com. http://www.architecture.com/go/Architecture/Home.html. Accessed October 10, 2004.

#58 Hendrick Medical Center
"History of Hendrick Medical Center." Hendrick Medical Center Website. http://www.ehendrick.org/history.htm. Accessed February 15, 2008.

#59 Caldwell Hall, Hardin-Simmons University
"Caldwell Hall Reborn." *Music Notes: The Annual Alumni Newsletter of the Hardin-Simmons School of Music.* Vol. 23 (March 2004). Available at
    http://www.hsutx.edu/academics/music/NewFiles/HSU_SOM_Alumni_04.pdf . Accessed February 23, 2008.

#60 Reese-Thornton House
Erinshire Website. http://www.erinshire.com/erinshire/index.html. Accessed February 22, 2008.
Myers, Doug. "Erinshire 'Dream' Up For Sale." *Abilene Reporter-News.* November 14, 2007.

#61 Sewell Theatre, Abilene Christian University
"ACU's History." Abilene Christian University Website. http://www.acu.edu/aboutacu/history.html. Accessed February 25, 2008.

#62 Zona Luce Building, Abilene Christian University
"ACU's History." Abilene Christian University Website. http://www.acu.edu/aboutacu/history.html. Accessed October 4, 2004.
City of Abilene. *Abilene Historic Landmarks.* Abilene, TX: City of Abilene. 1987; updated, 1990.
"Zona Luce Building To Be Rededicated." Abilene Christian University Website. http://www.acu.edu/people/news/zonaluce.html.
    Accessed February 19, 2008.

#63 Town and Country Drive-In Theater
Town and Country Drive-in Theater Website. http://www.towncountrydrivein.com. Accessed February 23, 2008.

#64 University Church of Christ
University Church of Christ Website. http://www.uccabilene.org/resources/history.htm. Accessed February 21, 2008.

#65 Woodson High School
Cortese, Micha. "Woodson's Proud Exes Hold Reunion." *Abilene Reporter-News,* July 6, 1996.
"Education for African-Americans in Abilene." http://cs1.mcm.edu/blackhistory/ed.htm. Accessed September 30, 2004.
Reed, Jerry Daniel. "Historical Marker Placed at Campus Built New in 1936 for Black Children." *Abilene Reporter-News.* March 7, 1997.

#66 Jordan Taylor and Company
Cosby, Hugh, ed. *The History of Abilene.* Abilene: Hugh E. Cosby Co., 1955.
Ellsworth, Ken. "Waldrop Known as Stalwart Business, Civic, Church Leader." *Abilene Reporter News.* May 8, 2007.
Jordan Taylor and Co. Website. http://www.jordantaylorandco.com/About%20us.htm. Accessed February 18, 2008.
Waldrop, Sam. Personal Interview with Michael Jerry Akin. November 12, 2004. Abilene, Texas.
Williamson, Doug. "Waldrop's Furniture Company Truly Caters to Customers." *Abilene Reporter News.* October 30, 1998.

#67 McLemore-Bass Building
City of Abilene. *Abilene Historic Landmarks.* Abilene, TX: City of Abilene. 1987; updated, 1990.
"History of McLemore-Bass Drug Co. No. One Store." Typewritten Report. Abilene Preservation League, Abilene, Texas).
Murphy, Brien. "Closing of Green Frog Gives Regulars the Blues," Reporter News Online.
    http://www.texnewsa.com/1998/2001/local/frog0607.html. Accessed November 15, 2004.

#68 Federal Building
"Texas-Taylor County." National Register of Historic Places Website. http://www.nationalhistoricalregister.com/TX/Taylor/state.html.
    Accessed February 26, 2008.

#69 Wooten Hotel
Borden, Melissa. "Building Targets High-end Tenants." *Abilene Reporter News.* August 8, 2004.
City of Abilene. *Abilene Historic Landmarks.* Abilene, TX: City of Abilene. 1987; updated, 1990.
Duff, Katharyn, with Betty Kay Seibt. *Catclaw Country.* Burnet, Texas: Eakin Press, 1980.
Shilcult, Tracy, David Coffey, and Donald S. Frazier. *Historic Abilene: An Illustrated History.* San Antonio: Historical Publishing Network, 2000.
Zachry, Juanita Daniel. *A Living History: Taylor County and the Big Country.* Abilene: Quality Printing, 1999.

#70 The Paramount Theatre
Paramount Theatre Website. http://www.paramount-abilene.org. Accessed February 23, 2008.

#71 First Baptist Church
"Baptist Building Costs $1,171,952." *Abilene Reporter News.* January 24, 1954.
"The Church Everlasting: Proposed Auditorium, First Baptist Church of Abilene, Texas." November 1950. First Baptist Church Library, Abilene, Texas.
Gray, J. Edward. "The History of the First Baptist Church of Abilene, Texas," Unpublished Master's Thesis (1957). Hardin-Simmons University, Abilene, Texas.
"Sanctuary Renovation, First Baptist Church of Abilene: Master Plan." March 2004. First Baptist Church Library, Abilene, Texas.

#72 Railway Express Agency Baggage Building (Candies by Vletas)
City of Abilene. *Abilene Historic Landmarks.* Abilene, TX: City of Abilene. 1987; updated, 1990.
Duff, Katharyn, with Betty Kay Seibt. *Catclaw Country.* Burnet, Texas: Eakin Press, 1980.
Wilson, Anthony. "Board Recommends Spending for Renovations of REA Baggage Express Building." *Abilene Reporter-News.* December 10, 1997.

#73 Coca-Cola Building
"ACU's History." Abilene Christian University Website. http://www.acu.edu/aboutacu/history.html. Accessed February 26, 2008.
McDaniel, Raymond. Interview with Robert F. Pace. February 26, 2008. Abilene, Texas.

#74 Borden Milk Company
"Borden Company." Funding Universe Website. http://www.fundinguniverse.com/company-histories/Borden-Inc-Company-History.html. Accessed February 23, 2008.

#75 Moreland-Shaheen House
Abilene Preservation League, "Architecture in Abilene: 2000 Calendar." 2000.
City of Abilene. *Abilene Historic Landmarks.* Abilene, TX: City of Abilene. 1987; updated, 1990.
Whitaker, Bill. "Sugar House." *Abilene Reporter News.* November 19, 1998.

#76 Frost-Grissom-Moore House
Abilene Register of Historic Properties. City of Abilene Website. http://www.abilenetx.com/historic/historic_register.htm. Accessed February 15, 2008.

#77 Church of the Heavenly Rest, Episcopal
Bratton, Conrad. Interview by Jim Jarrett, September 7, 2004. Abilene, Texas.
Smith, Jerry V. "Parish History." Church of the Heavenly Rest, Episcopal, Website. http://www.chrabilene.com/parish_history.htm. Accessed September 9, 2004.

#78 Sacred Heart Catholic Church
City of Abilene. *Abilene Historic Landmarks.* Abilene, TX: City of Abilene. 1987; updated, 1990.
Woodruff, Mark. *The Centennial History of Sacred Heart Church.* Abilene: R & R Printing and Reproductions, 2002.

#79 Dixie Pig
Varble, Sarah Kleiner. "It's Official: Dixie Pig is Historic Landmark." *Abilene Reporter-News.* October 30, 2007.

#80 Radford Building, McMurry University
Newman, Vernie. "A Sixty-Year History of McMurry College." 1986. Unpublished manuscript. McMurry University Archives, Abilene, Texas.
Sledge, Robert W. "McMurry Goes to War, 1940-1945." *Pride of Our Western Prairies: McMurry College, 1923-1988.* Ed. Fane Downs and Robert W. Sledge. Abilene: McMurry College, 1989.

#81 Abilene Courts
"Ready to Go? The Trip Starts at ...." *Abilene Reporter-News.* December 6, 2006.
    http://www.reporternews.com/abil/special_reports/article/0,1874,ABIL_8048_5219383,00.html. Accessed February 20, 2008.
"Highway 80." spiritus-temporis. http://www.spiritus-temporis.com/u.s.-highway-80/original-route.html. Accessed February 20, 2008.
"Highway 80." bygonebyways. 2001. bygonebyways.com. http://www.bygonebyways.com/Highway%2080.htm. Accessed February 20, 2008.
"US Highway 80 The Broadway of North America." gbcnet. http://gbcnet.com/ushighways/US80/US80.html. Accessed February 20, 2008.

#82 Shotwell Stadium
"Shotwell Stadium." AISD Website. http://www.aisd.org/information/facilities.asp#stadium. Accessed February 23, 2008.
"Shotwell Stadium." Wikipedia. http://en.wikipedia.org/wiki/Shotwell_Stadium. Accessed February 23, 2008.

#83 Hendrick Home for Children

Dahl, Barbara. Interview with Anders Jordan Leverton. February 16, 2008, Abilene, Texas.

"Hendrick Home for Children: Spiritual, Emotional, Physical, Intellectual." Pamphlet. Available at Hendrick Home for Children.

Tinney, Nora. Interview with Anders Jordan Leverton. February 16, 2008, Abilene, Texas.

#84 Dyess Air Force Base

"Dyess Air Force Base." Wikipedia. http://en.wikipedia.org/wiki/Dyess_Air_Force_Base#History. Accessed February 25, 2008.

#85 Wal-Mart Supercenter

CNN.com. http://money.cnn.com/magazines/fortune/global500/2007/. Accessed February 23, 2008.

"Wal-Mart Coming to North Abilene." ACU Optimist. http://media.www.acuoptimist.com/media/storage/paper891/news/2004/09/08/News/WalMart.Coming.To.North.Abilene-2429652.shtml. Accessed February 23, 2008.

#86 Crutcher Scott Field, Abilene Christian University

"Crutcher Scott Field." Abilene Christian University Website. http://www.acu.edu/sports/baseball/crutcher_scott.html. Accessed 15 February 2008.

#87 Logsdon Chapel, Hardin-Simmons University

Stone, James. Interview with Gail Adlesperger. February 18, 2008. Abilene, Texas.

#88 Abilene Civic Center

"Abilene Civic Center." City of Abilene Website. http://www.abilenetx.com/CivicCenter/index.htm. Accessed February 21, 2008.

#89 First Christian Church

Hurley, Jane, Director of Christian Education and Evangelism at First Christian Church of Abilene. Email to Ben Newland. February 25, 2008.

#90 Frontier Texas!

Frontier Texas! Website. http://www.frontiertexas.com/pressroom.html. Accessed February 14, 2008.

#91 Taco Bueno

"Taco Bueno." Wikipedia. http://en.wikipedia.org/wiki/Taco_Bueno. Accessed February 23, 2008.

#92 Enterprise Building

"Summary of Salient Facts, Data, and Conclusions," Report of the West Texas Appraisal Association. September 10, 1996.

#93 Taylor County Courthouse

"Taylor County Courthouse." Texas Escapes Online Magazine. http://www.texasescapes.com/TOWNS/Abilene/Taylor-County-Courthouse-Abilene-Texas.htm. Accessed February 20, 2008.

#94 Abilene Zoological Gardens

Abilene Zoo Website. http://www.abilenetx.com/zoo/index.htm. Accessed February 24, 2008.

McDonald, Donald. Interview with Robert Pace. February 24, 2008. Abilene, Texas.

#95 Taylor County Expo Center

Taylor County Expo Center Website. http://www.taylorcountyexpocenter.com/. Accessed February 23, 2008.

#96 Cisco Junior College

"Cisco Junior College." Wikipedia. http://en.wikipedia.org/wiki/Cisco_Junior_College. Accessed February 23, 2008.

#97 Abilene Regional Medical Center

Abilene Regional Medical Center Website. http://www.abileneregional.com. Accessed February 17, 2008.

Leverton, Robert S., II., M.D. Interview with Anders Jordan Leverton. February 16, 2008. Abilene, Texas.

#98 Wesley Court Retirement Center

Wesley Court Retirement Center Website. http://www.sears-methodist.com/ret_comm/wesleycourt/index2.htm. Accessed February 19, 2008.

#99 Wylie United Methodist Church

"Gatlin Brothers-Southwest Golf Classic." Wikipedia. http://en.wikipedia.org/wiki/Gatlin_Brothers-Southwest_Golf_Classic. Accessed February 21, 2008.

Wylie United Methodist Church Website. http://www.wyliemethodist.org/aboutus.htm. Accessed February 21, 2008.

#100 Mall of Abilene

Majors, Steve. Interview with Anders Jordan Leverton. February 18, 2008. Abilene, Texas.

Mall of Abilene Website. http://www.mallofabilene.com/. Accessed February 20, 2008.

244

245